A _Texas_ SAMPLER

A Texas SAMPLER

HISTORICAL RECOLLECTIONS

LISA WALLER ROGERS

TEXAS TECH UNIVERSITY PRESS

This book was set in Americana and Commercial Script.

The paper used in this book meets the minimum requirements of ANSI/NISO Z39.48-1992 (R1997). ∞

Design by Melissa Bartz

Printed in Hong Kong

Library of Congress Cataloging-in-Publication Data
A Texas sampler : historic recollections / [compiled by] Lisa Waller   Rogers.
        p.   cm.
    Includes bibliographical references and index.
    ISBN 0-89672-393-3 (acid-free paper)
    1. Texas—History—To 1846—Sources. 2. Ethnology—Texas—
    History—Sources. 3. Pluralism (Social sciences)—Texas—
    History—Sources. I. Rogers, Lisa Waller, 1955-
    F389.T375 1998
    976.4—dc21   98-24589
                                                     CIP

99 00 01 02 03 04 05 06 / 9 8 7 6 5 4 3 2

Texas Tech University Press
Box 41037
Lubbock, Texas 79409-1037 USA

1-800-832-4042

ttup@ttu.edu

Preface

Remember the old parlor game, "Telephone"? Everybody sits in a circle. The leader begins by whispering a message in a neighbor's ear. That person whispers it to the next. This continues until the message makes its way around the circle. When the last person receives the whispered message, he or she announces it to the group. At this point, everybody laughs. The last message does not even resemble the first.

Much the same thing happens with history. With each telling and retelling, stories from our past undergo transformation. Pieces can get lost or changed. Meaning can become twisted. To get at the truth, one must sometimes return to the ore from which our current history is mined—firsthand accounts.

Firsthand accounts, though, have their own problems. The excerpts from authentic diaries, letters, journals, and memoirs that are found in *A Texas Sampler* were written by real people who lived in a different time than we do. Some were prejudiced and their writing reflects their bias. Some were uneducated and their writing can be riddled with incorrect spelling, capitalization, and grammar. The excerpts appear exactly as they were written. The few changes that were made were done to clarify meaning and are enclosed by square brackets.

By today's standards, some of these passages may be considered offensive. Even so, each passage offers us insight into a time gone by, a time when Indians roamed this great state looking for buffalo and barefoot children fished in crystal clear creeks. These tales were not written by me. They were written by the remarkable people who settled Texas—for you.

To My Texas Grandfathers,
John Andrew Waller, Sr. (1902–1997)
and
Jesse Thwing King (1905–1991).
Their greatness lay in their simple,
old-fashioned devotion to God and family.

Contents

List of Illustrations

Unit One
SILVER BARS AND CUTLASSES

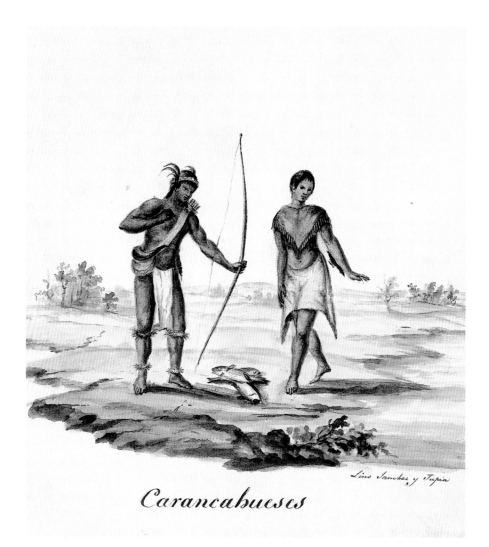

Carancahueses

In this sketch, two Carancahua Indians look like mannequins from an early eighteenth-century European fashion plate (Lino Sánchez y Tapía, *Carancahueses*, watercolor, ca. 1830, From the Collection of Gilcrease Museum, Tulsa, Oklahoma).

Chapter 1
THE WEEPERS AND THE WAILERS

Alvar Núñez Cabeza de Vaca (ca. 1490–ca. 1557) explored Texas long before the English landed at Plymouth Rock. But he had not meant to visit Texas. Treasurer of the Narváez Expedition, he had been sent from Spain to look for gold in Florida. But his expedition was snake-bitten. Hurricanes, hostile Indians, hunger, and sickness sabotaged his plans. After a year and a half of wandering the Mississippi River Valley and the Gulf of Mexico, Cabeza de Vaca and fifty other ragged and naked men were shipwrecked off the Texas coast on Galveston Island.

They were found on the beach by the Carancahua Indians, who looked like giants to the frightened Spaniards. The white men prepared to be eaten. Instead, the Carancahuas, taken aback to see their fellow humans in such a pitiful state, began to weep. Once the sobs died down, the Indians carried the shivering men over to a fire to be warmed. Then they fed them roots and fish and built them a hut.

Here is Cabeza de Vaca's description of the Carancahuas, who vanished shortly after the coming of the white man to Texas.

The people we came to know there are tall and well built. Their only weapons are bows and arrows, which they use with great dexterity. The men bore through one of their nipples, some both, and insert a joint of cane two and a half palms long by two fingers thick. They also bore their lower lip and wear a piece of cane in it half a finger in diameter.

Their women toil incessantly.

From October to the end of February every year, which is the season these Indians live on the island, they subsist on the roots I have mentioned, which the women get from under water in November and December. Only in these two months, too, do they take fish in their cane weirs. When the fish is consumed, the roots furnish the one staple. At the end of February the islanders go into other parts to seek sustenance, for then the root is beginning to grow and is not edible.

These people love their offspring more than any in the world and treat them.very mildly.

If a son dies, the whole village joins the parents and kindred in weeping. The parents set off the wails each day before dawn, again at noon, and at sunset, for one year. The funeral rites occur when the year of mourning is up. Following these rites, the survivors wash off the smoke stain of the ceremony in a symbolic purgation. All the dead are lamented this way except the aged, who merit no regrets. The dead are buried, except medicine men, who are cremated. Everybody in the village dances and makes merry while the pyre of a medicine man kindles, and until his bones become powder. A year later, when his rites are celebrated, the entire village again participating, this powder is presented in water for the relatives to drink.

Each man has an acknowledged wife, except the medicine men, who may have two or three wives apiece. The several wives live together in perfect amity.

When a daughter marries, she must take everything her husband kills in hunting or catches in fishing to the house of her father, without daring to eat or to withhold any part of it, and the husband gets provided by female carrier from his father-in-law's house. Neither the bride's father nor mother may enter the son-in-law's house after the marriage, nor he theirs; and this holds for the children of the respective couples. If a man and his in-laws should chance to be walking so they would meet, they turn silently aside from each other and go a crossbow-shot out of their way, averting their glance to the ground. The woman, however, is free to fraternize with the parents and relatives of her husband. . . .

At a house where a son or brother may die, no one goes out for food for three months, the neighbors and other relatives providing what is eaten. Because of this custom, which the Indians literally would not break to save their lives, great hunger reigned in most houses while we resided there, it being a time of repeated deaths. . . .

Three months out of every year they eat nothing but oysters and drink very bad water. Wood is scarce; mosquitoes, plentiful. The houses are made of mats; their floors consist of masses of oyster shells. The natives sleep on these shells—in animal skins, those who happen to own such.

Many a time I would have to go three days without eating, as would the natives. I thought it impossible that life could be so prolonged in such protracted hunger. . . .

The inhabitants of all these parts go naked, except that the women cover some part of their persons with a wool that grows on trees [Spanish moss], and damsels dress in deerskin.

The people are generous to each other with what little they have. There is no chief. All belonging to the same lineage keep together. They speak two languages: Capoque and Han.

They have a strange custom when acquaintances meet or occasionally visit, of weeping for half an hour before they speak. This over, the one who is visited rises and gives his visitor all he has. The latter accepts it and, after a while, carries it away, often without a word. They have other strange customs, but I have told the principal and most remarkable of them.

From The Journey of Alvar Núñez Cabeza de Vaca, translated by Fanny Bandelier, Rio Grande Press, 1905. Reprinted courtesy of AMS Press.

This huge painting (7 by 9½ feet) was commissioned by the cousin of the slain priest shown at left (José de Paez, *The Destruction of Mission San Sabá in the Province of Texas and the Martyrdom of the Fathers Alonso Giraldo de Terreros, Joseph Santiesteban*, oil, 1763, Museo Nacional de Arte, Mexico City). (TR: 143-90) Photograph courtesy of the Museum of Fine Arts, Houston; lent by agreement with the United States Custom Service.

Chapter 2
THE MISSION SAN SABÁ

[I was] filled with amazement and fear when I saw nothing
but Indians on every hand, armed with guns and arrayed in
the most horrible attire. Besides the paint on their faces, red
and black, they were adorned with the pelts and tails of wild
beasts, wrapped around them or hanging down from their
heads, as well as deer horns. Some were disguised as various kinds of animals, and some wore feather headdresses.
All were armed with muskets, swords, and lances, and I noticed also that they had brought with them some youths
armed with bows and arrows.

—Friar Miguel de Molina,
in a report on the San Sabá Massacre, March 22, 1758

*They came talking peace but dressed for war. Two thousand
Comanche warriors on horseback surrounded the tiny Mission
San Sabá that March morning in 1758. The chiefs approached the
gate. In broken Spanish, they promised the guards that they had
not come to harm the Spanish. It was only the Apaches who were
their enemies.*

*Reluctantly, the guards let them in. The Franciscan padres
rushed out to welcome the chiefs with tobacco and trinkets, hop-
ing to forestall the inevitable. But all was lost. Within minutes, the
huge force attacked, decapitating Father Santiesteban, shooting
Father Terreros, murdering almost all the other inhabitants, mutilat-
ing the cats and cows, and burning the whole place to the ground.*

*It had been a cockeyed notion from the beginning, sticking an
unprotected mission in the heart of the Comanchería. But there
was more to this little log village than bringing the Apaches to*

Jesus. After all, Spanish dreams of golden cities did not die when Coronado left Texas.

Don Bernardo de Miranda had officially explored the San Sabá Valley two years earlier at the request of the Spanish governor of Texas. His findings, detailed in his reports, reveal the true "mission" of the Mission San Sabá. Here are a few excerpts.

The mines that are throughout the Cerro del Almagre [Hill of Red Ore] and all its slope are so abundant that I guarantee to give a mine to each one of all the inhabitants of this province of Texas. . . .

Of the conveniences, not the least are the large and nearby thickets of mesquite and oak, very useful for charcoal. For house building and other necessities needed by *haciendas* for extracting silver, there is much cedar, pecan, cottonwood, and oak timber; and also, wherever they want to open them, [there are] rock quarries for houses and for lime. . . .

Although I would have liked to have fulfilled my obligation to see and explore all the land of the Apaches, I had no means for the reasons stated, nor did I find any Indian of the Apache nation who would guide me so that I could make other discoveries. In order to succeed in encountering some [Indians], I made use of the scheme of setting fire to the field at several places, but this scheme did not produce the desired result until, on the way back, on the Río de Alarcón, a well-known Apache Indian overtook me. He gave me reason to believe that at the source of the Río Colorado, six days journey beyond what I had seen, there were two good deposits of *almagre* that were those they took from for their use, and that four more days' journey from these two *almagres* was another with two rich ore veins; but in order to go to this one, many Spaniards would be needed. They, together with the

Apaches, could go; because if only a few go and the Comanche Indians are living at this *almagre*, [the Comanches] could kill them all.

Telling him that I wanted to paint churches and houses [with *almagre* dye], I offered him a blanket, some tobacco, a horse, a bridle, a big knife, and other trifles if he would take me to the *almagres*, because the one that I had seen was no good. I used this pretext so that he would not guess the real reason. He gave me his word to conduct me whenever I wanted, and if we came every "moon" he would travel with the Spaniards. For this I used the interpreter whom I took along. . . .

[M]ost of the [silver] veins run from east to west and some from north to south . . . the principal vein is more than 2 *varas* thick. . . .

According to the statement of the Apache Indians, many more and better mines can be discovered at the source of the Río Colorado, and many also in the place where the Comanche Indians are found; for the two pockets of ore that are mentioned . . . are not ore but silver according to the assertion of the Apache Indians, who explained themselves by telling me that they are white like shoe buckles.

But it is to be . . . kept in mind . . . that the . . . mines . . . cannot be worked as long as a presidio of at least thirty men to restrain the Indians is not established. . . .

And in case Your Excellency does not regard this proposition to be to your superior liking, I am ready to pay all of it through my industry and perseverance with the condition that I be the captain of the soldiers that are found to be placed at the said mines. . . . Thus equipped I will be able to assist those who work the mines so that all will be given in the service of His Majesty, augmenting his royal purse and benefiting the public until there are sufficient residents to defend themselves from the assaults of the Indians.

Bernardo de Miranda

Reprinted with permission from Southwestern Historical Quarterly, *Vol. 1. LXXIV (1970-1971), courtesy of Texas State Historical Association, Austin.*

In 1817, Jean Lafitte, known as "the Pirate of the Gulf," made Galveston Island his headquarters (Artist unknown, *Jean Lafitte*, Prints and Photographs Collection, CN 00882, The Center for American History, University of Texas at Austin).

Chapter 3
THE GHOST OF JEAN LAFITTE

Stories have been circulated . . . that I have hidden silver and gold on the sandy islands all along the Gulf Coast. . . .

It is true. There are things hidden here and there. . . .
When I am dead my spirit will hover near and witness.

—Jean Lafitte, from his journal, 1850

There is an old, broken-down house in La Porte, Texas, that local people swear is haunted. Under that house, so they say, is treasure buried by the Pirate of the Gulf, Jean Lafitte, and his buccaneers. Guarding the booty, the legend runs, is the troubled spirit of Lafitte himself. It is said that anyone foolish enough to spend a night alone in that house will be visited by his ghost.

The Texas historian and folklorist J. Frank Dobie talked to many people familiar with this legend. The following experience was related to him by a Confederate war veteran, no longer living, whom he dubbed "Major Walcart," though that was not his real name.

It was on a February night back in the [eighteen] eighties. The early darkness of a murky day had overtaken me, and I was dead tired. I do not think mud ever lay deeper along the shore of Galveston Bay, or that an east wind ever blew more bleakly. When I came to a small stream I rode out into the open water, as the custom then was, to find shallow passage. A full moon was rising out of the bay. Heavy clouds stretched just above it, and I remember the unearthly aspect of the blustering breakers in its cheerless light. The immensity and unfriendliness of the scene made me feel lonesome, and I think the horse shared my mood. By common consent we turned across before we had gone far enough from shore, and fell into the trench cut by the stream in the bottom of the bay.

We were wretchedly wet as we scrambled up a clayey slope and gained the top of the bluff. A thin cry which I had not been sure was real when I first heard it now became insistent. It was like the wail of a child in mortal pain, and I confess that it reminded me of tales I had heard of the werewolf, which lures unwary travelers to their doom by imitating the cry of a human infant. By the uncertain light of the moon, which the next moment was cut off entirely, I saw that I had reached a kind of stable that crowned the bluff, and from this structure the uncanny summons seemed to come.

The sounds were growing fainter, and I hesitated but a moment. Dismounting, I led my horse through the doorless entrance, and now the mystery was explained. Huddled together for warmth lay a flock of sleeping goats. A kid had rashly squeezed itself into the middle of the heap, and the insensate brutes were rushing its life out. I found the perishing little creature, and its flattened body came back to the full tide of life in my arms. Its warmth was grateful to my cold fingers, and I fondled it a moment before setting it down on the dry dirt floor.

I tied my horse to a post that upheld the roof of the stable, and with saddle and blanket on my arm started toward the house, which I could make out in its quadrangle of oaks, not many yards distant. The horse whinnied protestingly as I left him, and when the moaning of the wind in the eaves smote my ears I was half in mind to turn back and bunk with the goats. It was a more forbidding sound than the hostile roar of the breakers had been in the bay.

I called, but only the muddy waves incessantly tearing at the bluff made answer. I had scarcely hoped really to hear the sound of a human voice. The great double doors leading in from the front porch were barred, but the first window I tried yielded entrance. Striking a match, I found myself in a room that gave promise of comfort. Fat pine kindling lay beside the big fireplace, and dry chunks of solid oak were waiting to glow for me the whole night through.

I was vaguely conscious that the brave fire I soon had going did not drive the chill from the air so promptly as it should, but my head was too heavy with sleep to be bothered. I spread my horse blanket quite close to the cheerful blaze, and with saddle for pillow and slicker for cover I abandoned myself to the luxury of rest.

I do not know how long I had slept when I became aware of a steady gaze fixed on my face. The man was looking down on me, and no living creature ever stood so still. There was impervious command in the unblinking eyes, and yet I saw a sort of profound entreaty also.

It was plain that the visitant had business with me. I arose, and together we left the room, passed its neighbor, and entered a third, a barren little apartment through whose cracks the wind came mercilessly. I think it was I who had opened the doors. My companion did not seem to move. He was merely present all the time.

"It is here," he said, as I halted in the middle of the bare floor, "that more gold lies buried than is good for any man. You have but to dig, and it is yours. You can use it; I cannot. However, it must be applied only to purposes of highest beneficence. Not one penny may be evilly or selfishly spent. On this point you must keep faith and beware of any failing. Do you accept?"

I answered, "Yes," and the visitant was gone, and I was shivering with cold. I groped my way back to my fire, bumping into obstructions I had not found in my journey away from it. I piled on wood with a generous hand, and the flames leaped high. I watched the unaccountable shadows dance on the whitewashed walls, and marked how firebeams flickered across the warpings of the boards in the floor. Then I dozed off.

I do not know how long I had been asleep when I felt the presence of the visitant again. The still reproach of his fixed eyes was worse than wrath. "I need your help more than you can know," he said, "and you would fail me. The treasure is mine to give. I paid for it with the substance of my soul. I want you to have it. With it you can balance somewhat the burden of guilt I carry for its sake."

Again we made the journey to the spot where the treasure was buried, and this time he showed it to me. There were yellow coins, jeweled watches, women's bracelets, diamond rings, and strings of pearls. It was just such a trove as I had dreamed of when as a boy I had planned to dig for Lafitte's treasure except that the quantity of it was greater. With the admonition, "Do not force me to come again," my companion was gone, and once more I made my way back to the fire.

This time I took up my saddle and blanket and went out to the company of my horse. The wind and the waves were wailing together, but I thought I saw a promise of light across the chilly bay, and never was the prospect of dawn more welcome. As I saddled up and rode off, the doleful boom of the muddy water at the foot of the bluff came to me like an echoed anguish.

"The Uneasy Ghost of Lafitte," Julia Beazley. From Legends of Texas, Vol. II., *J. Frank Dobie (ed.). Used by permission of the publisher, Pelican Publishing Company, Inc. Copyright 1924 by J. Frank Dobie. Reprinted from original edition by permission of the Texas Folklore Society.*

Interestingly, no reason has ever been given as to why the treasure was not taken.

Unit Two

GONE TO TEXAS

1ère Vue d'Aigleville, Colonie du Texas ou Champ d'Asile

Occupations des nouveaux Colons, Fort Henri, chemin couvert qui mène au fort et habitation d'un Colon.

Champ d'Asile, founded in 1817 on the Trinity River, was a settlement of Napoleonic exiles (Louis Garneray, *1ère Vue d'Aigleville Colonie du Texas ou Champ d'Asile [First view of the Eagleville Colony of Texas or Camp Asylum]*, engraving, 1830, courtesy of Library of Congress, reproduction number LC-USZ6Z-38606).

Chapter 4
BLACK PELICAN SOUP

In the engraving shown here, a smartly dressed French family has its first look at the Champ d'Asile colony, founded along the Trinity River in January 1817. Even though they have just stepped off a boat, the group is fresh and carefree. All their needs are being met without a single one of them lifting a finger. Pineapples and bananas tumble from a nearby basket, a pot of stew magically cooks itself, and wooden homes and stone defenses go up around them while they relax in the shade.

This French family never existed. Real immigrants, newly arrived on Texas shores, would hardly qualify for the fashion pages of Vogue. *The journey to Texas was arduous, especially the voyage across the choppy Gulf of Mexico, and it took its toll.*

Mary Wightman Helm was a bride of eighteen when she came to Matagorda, Texas, in 1829. She traveled by wagon, flatboat, raft, and steamboat to get from New York to New Orleans. From there, she took a schooner to Texas. Here is her account of that Gulf crossing.

The usual time for sailing from New Orleans to Texas was seven days, so we only took provisions for sixty persons for seven days, and about the time that was consumed our water also became alarmingly scarce—half a pint a day to each person. Being sick, I could not drink the water, nor the tea and coffee made from it. A little vinegar and sugar, diluted with this bad water, sustained me. There were no conveniences for cooking, except a stationary sheet-iron boiler, so-called, in which we were allowed to heat water for our tea and coffee.

Our Captain, one day, very kindly volunteered to make it full of vegetable soup for all the passengers, when we, or more especially the well ones, were nearly famished, and invited his sixty passengers to help themselves. And such a scrambling! It would have made a picture for Harper [*Harper's* magazine]. Many could not procure vessels to get what they so much needed. It so happened that a small tin cup fell to my lot; it was very small at the top and took a long time to cool. I had been nine days without food and but very little to drink, because I could not eat and drink such as the vessel afforded, and having a fever did not crave much. Now came the tug of war. Those who could procure large vessels took too much. By the time I had cooled and consumed my gift of soup the boiler was empty. Looking down the hatchway I saw a family of three with a six-quart pan full, and reaching down my cup, I requested them to fill it. They parleyed and said they could not spare any. I would not report, to make trouble for my friends; but after I had retired in disgust they offered to fill my cup. I do not remember the sequel, only remember telling them of it years after, at which time, of course, they had forgotten the circumstance.

After our cooked provisions had given out, crackers and hard sea bread sustained life; but when the water gave out, then real suffering commenced. And such water! I really supposed then that powder casks had been used for holding the water, not having learned then that it took time for water to become good. The well passengers could drink it made into coffee, but it so affected me that I could not endure the smell of coffee for several years. Mr. Pilgrim says that he gave his share of the water to the children, and sustained himself on whiskey and crackers.

Some of our men had the good fortune to shoot and kill a pelican, a most disgusting sea fowl that lives on fish, having a large pouch in front that holds his prey till time of need. Its flesh is black and tastes fishy. I had not tasted food for so many days, that I was constantly dreaming of soups and milk, or something to sustain life. We had a little sick boy, Laroy Griffeth, now more than sixty years of age, who also craved food. The bird was boiled and the boy promised the meat, but I not caring for the meat, craved the soup, worth more to me than its weight in gold. When, to my astonishment, the boy was in tears for fear "Aunt Mary would eat all the meat," while I was about as foolish about the soup.

We had, a few days before, witnessed a burial at sea, and we naturally felt that unless relief came soon, it would be repeated. This was the first time I had ever experienced *want*—want of something to sustain life—and no wonder I worshipped the disgusting soup of the pelican, so that when a hurricane drove us into Aransas Bay, no wonder we did not think of Indians. And now, again, as we enter Matagorda Pass, Sunday morning, January 27, 1829, with all our fears of hostile Indians, whose telegraphic smokes told of our approach, a joyful thankfulness filled our heart, for we were entering the land of promise. . . .

[O]ur friends on land sent out our poor weary and worn immigrants a sumptuous dinner on board the vessel . . . of boiled hominy, pounded in a mortar, cooked meats of various kinds, also a variety of fish and fowl, and a large bucket of sweet milk and some sweet potatoes. . . . Our sixty starving sea-worn passengers were thus welcomed to their long sought for post, after an absence of thirty-one days from New Orleans.

Scraps of Early Texas History, *Mary Sherwood Helm, Austin, privately printed, 1884. Reprinted in* Texas Tears and Sunshine: Voices of Frontier Women, *Jo Ella Powell Exley (ed.), Texas A&M Press, 1985. Reprinted courtesy of Texas A&M Press.*

Texas Indians called the bluebonnet "a gift from the Great Spirit" (Robert Julian Onderdonk, *Bluebonnet Field*, oil, 1912, Witte Museum, San Antonio, Texas).

Chapter 5
THE GARDEN SPOT OF THE WORLD

In August of 1821, Stephen F. Austin secured a colonization grant from the Mexican government. For the rest of that summer, Austin traveled through Texas, surveying, looking for the perfect site for his colony. He found just the spot. It was in the southern coastal plains, close to the Gulf of Mexico, where rainfall was plentiful. It lay just outside of dangerous Comanche territory. The tract was the rich Brazos River bottomland, first-rate land for Southern cotton planters. Austin had the grant and the land; now he needed settlers.

The young empresario left Texas for Louisiana to run more newspaper advertisements to stir up interest in his colony. As it turned out, this was unnecessary. When he arrived at Natchitoches, he found about a hundred letters from men and women hungry for Texas land. The letters continued to pour in. The word was out. Texas was the Land of Promise.

Texas fever swept across the United States during the 1820s and 1830s. Immigrants surged westward to set up farms and seek their fortunes. Land was the lure and this land was enchanting. Davy Crockett, in the last letter he ever wrote, describes to his children the uncommon beauty he found in Texas.

Saint Agustine Texas

9th January 1836

My dear Sone & daughter,

This is the first I have had an oportunity to write to you with convenience. I am now blessed with excellent health and am in high spirits although I have had many difficulties to encounter. I have got through safe and have been received by everybody with the open cerimony of friendship.

I am hailed with a harty welcome to this country. A dinner and a party of ladys have honored me with an invitation to partisapate with them both at Nacogdoches and this place. The Cannon was fired here on my arivel and I must say as to what I have seen of Texas it [is] the garden spot of the world the best land and the best prospects for health I ever saw and I do believe it is a fortune to any man to come here. There is a world of country here to settle.

It is not required here to pay down for your League of land—every man is entitled to his headright of 4438 acres—they may make the money to pay for it on the land. I expect in all probilaty to settle on the Bordar or Chactow Bio [bayou] of Red River that I have no doubt is the richest country in the world—good land and plenty of timber and the best springs & good mill streams good range clear water—and every appearance of good health and game plenty—It is in the pass whare the Buffalo passes from North to South and back twice a year—and bees and honey plenty—I have a great hope of getting the agency to settle that country and I would be glad to see every friend I have settled there. It would be a fortune to them all.

I have taken the oath of government and have enrolled my name as a volunteer for six months and will set out for the Rio grand in a few days with the volunteers from the United States. But all volunteers is intitled to a vote for a member to the convention or to be voted for and I have but little doubt of being elected a member to form a Constitution for this province. I am rejoiced at my fate. I had rather be in my present situation than to be elected to a seat in Congress for life. I am in hopes of making a fortune yet for myself and family bad as my prospect has been.

I have not wrote to William, but have requested John to direct him what to do. I hope you show him this letter and also Brother John as it is not convenient at this time for me to write to them. I hope you will all do the best you can and I will do the same. Do not be uneasy about me. I am among my friends—I must close. With great respects to Wiley & Margaret Flowers.

Your affectionate father.

Farewell.

David Crockett

Reprinted with permission from the Special Collections Library of the University of Tennessee, Knoxville.

Indian attacks on the Texas frontier were a constant danger (J. M. Boundy, *The Weak Never Started, October 19, 1861,* Jack S. Blanton Museum of Art, the University of Texas at Austin. Bequest of C. R. Smith, 1991. Photo credit, George Holmes).

Chapter 6
THE WEAK NEVER STARTED

For those who came to Texas in covered wagons, the journey was long and hard. On a good day, when the wheels did not get stuck in mud, the wagons traveled ten to fifteen miles, stopping to camp just before dark. These pioneers did not travel alone; they knew there was strength in numbers. Great wagon caravans stretched for miles across the prairie followed by a steady stream of livestock—mules, cows, sheep, hogs, and extra horses—many of which would become food along the way.

The emigrants left home optimistic—and well-prepared. They loaded up their wagons with bacon and beans, cornmeal and salt, shovels and axes, seeds, candle molds, bolts of calico, rifles, tea-kettles, chamber pots, rocking chairs, and, of course, the family Bible. Few stores existed along the uncertain path that led from Natchitoches, Louisiana, across the Sabine River and down to San Antonio. The pioneers wanted to be ready for any challenge they might encounter.

Despite this careful planning, though, many of them never made it. Scores of people were swept from wagons and drowned as they tried to cross swollen, fast-moving rivers. Others fell prey to cholera and "yellow jack," diseases that traveled with lightning speed and had no cures. The Texas blue northers and the burning summer heat often proved too intense for the newcomers. And always lurking along the open road was the threat of a vicious Indian attack. The trail to Texas was lined with graves of emigrants, many of whom met their deaths by tomahawk.

In 1837, Mary Maverick left her home in Tuscaloosa, Alabama, and journeyed by wagon train to Texas. In the following memoir,

she recalls a chance encounter with Tonkawas along the trail be-
tween Goliad and San Antonio.

June 12th, late in the afternoon, we reached camp again, and were loading up to move on two or three miles further to a better camping place for the night, when several Indians rode up. They said, "Mucho Amigo," (dear friend) and were loud and filthy and manifested their intention to be very intimate. More and more came until we counted seventeen! They rode in amongst us, looked constantly at the horses, and it is no exaggeration to say, they annoyed us very much.

They were Tonkawas, said they were just in from a battle, in which they were victors, on the Nueces River, where they had fought the Comanches two days before. They were in war paint, and well armed, and displayed in triumph two scalps, one hand, and several pieces of putrid flesh from various parts of the human body. These were to be taken to the squaws to eat and dance around when these warriors rejoined the tribe.

I was frightened almost to death, but tried not to show my alarm. They rode up to the carriage window and asked to see the "papoose." First one, then another came, and I held up my little Sammy, and smiled at their complaints. But I took care to have my pistol and bowie knife visible, and kept cool, and declined most decidedly when they asked me to hand the baby out to them that they might "see how pretty and white" he was.

I knew, and so did we all, though we did not tell each other till afterwards, that they, being cannibals, would like to eat my baby, and kill us all and carry off our horses. But we had six men fully armed and determined and all hands kept steadily loading the wagons, saddling the horses and preparing to move. I kept telling Griffin to hurry the others, and Mr. Maverick worked coolly with the rest. Jinny said, "Let's cook some supper first," and grumbled mightily when Griffin ordered her into the wagon and drove off.

Imagine our consternation when the Indians turned back, and every one of the seventeen rode along with us! It was a bright moonlight night, and Griffin and one other on horseback acted as our rear guard. About midnight, some of the Indians, finding we were so unsociable and seeing that we were dangerous, commenced dropping behind, and one by one they turned back, until at early dawn, when we reached the Cibolo, having travelled eighteen miles during the night, only two Indians were still attendant. Here we camped and the two Indians sat down, not far off, in an observant attitude.

I went into my tent to lie down, and Griffin said, "Don't be afraid, Miss Mary, but go to sleep," and I saw him sit down in front of the tent, with his gun, and an ax in his hands which he shook at the Indians, and said: "Come this way if you dare, you devils, and I'll make hash out of you!" I went to sleep with the baby and when I waked, all the vile Indians were gone, everybody rested, and my breakfast and dinner were both waiting for me. That certainly was a narrow escape from a cruel death.

From Memoirs of Mary A. Maverick, *Rena Maverick Green* (ed.), University of Nebraska Press, 1989.

A Mississippi flatboat was "the poor man's transfer" to a new life in Texas (George Caleb Bingham, *The Jolly Flatboatmen*, oil, 1846, Manoogian Foundation).

Chapter 7
THE JOLLY FLATBOATMEN

Flatboating to New Orleans was often one of the first steps in the journey for settlers bound for Texas. In 1827, Noah Smithwick boarded a Mississippi River flatboat, having left his native Tennessee to seek his fortune in the "lazy man's paradise," Texas. Here is his story.

I was but a boy in my nineteenth year, and in for adventure. My older brothers talked of going. They, however, abandoned the project; but, it had taken complete possession of me, so early in the following year, 1827, I started out from Hopkinsville, Kentucky, with all my worldly possessions, consisting of a few dollars in money, a change of clothes, and a gun, of course, to seek my fortune in this lazy man's paradise.

Incredible as it may seem to the present generation, seeing the country traversed from ocean to ocean and lakes to gulf with innumerable lines of railroad, there was not then a mile of railroad in operation in the United States; and though twenty years had elapsed since the Clermont made her triumphal trip from New York to Albany, few steamboats plied the western waters and none had ventured out to sea. I saw the first one that went up the Cumberland River—the Rifleman, a sternwheeler. Its progress was so slow that one had to take sight by stationary objects to determine if it moved.

The stage coach, being the only public overland conveyance, took me down to the mouth of the river, where I intended to take steamer for New Orleans; but the steamboat had not arrived and no one knew when it would: My impatience could brook no delay, so I took passage on a flatboat, or as they were know in river parlance, a "Mississippi broadhorn," the poor man's transfer. Out on the broad bosom of the Father of Waters these boats floated from the Ohio, the Cumberland, the Tennessee, and numerous smaller tributaries, laden with the products of the vast region contiguous, to be floated down to New Orleans and thence distributed around the seaboard by sailing vessels. The flatboat having served its purpose, it was broken up and sold for lumber and fuel, while the owner pocketed his cash and wended his way home, generally on foot up through Mississippi, where he was liable to be interviewed by footpads and relieved of his money if not his life. Many were the gruesome stories of robbery and murder thus committed by old John A. Murrill and his band of freebooters.

My transport was loaded with ice, artificial ice being a thing unheard of.* The crew consisted of three men, whose principal duty was to look out for "sawyers," sunken trees, and to keep clear of eddies, for a boat once drawn into the swirl would go floating around indefinitely, in danger of colliding with the ever-accumulating drift and being sunk.

As flatboats never returned and seldom passed each other, the slow, leisurely drifting, day after day, became intolerably monotonous. So I stopped off at Natchez and waited for a steamboat. Very poetical it was, no doubt, this dropping down with the rippling stream, but I had not started out in search of the poetical.

From Evolution of a State, Noah Smithwick, University of Texas Press, 1983. Reprinted with permission of the University of Texas Press.

*Artificial ice refers to ice manufactured in factories. The first ice factory opened in New Orleans in 1868. The ice on this flatboat was probably cut in chunks from a northern lake, packed in hay, and sent downriver.

Chapter 8
THE MURDERS OF HAGGETT AND WILLIAMS

In the painting The Settlement of Austin's Colony, *Stephen F. Austin is shown in his headquarters at San Felipe de Austin busily issuing land titles. His work is interrupted by the sudden entrance of a scout. The newcomer, his headband stained with blood, points upriver to burning cabins in the distance. The Carancahuas were up to their devilish work again. Instinctively, Stephen Austin reaches for his rifle.*

Mr. Austin eventually made peace with the Carancahuas and a lasting treaty was signed in 1827. In that same year, he established his second colony, east of the Colorado River and north of the Camino Real. It became known as Austin's "Little Colony." The tiny town of Bastrop was chosen as its capital.

Being situated so far west and isolated, the Little Colony was plagued by Comanche attack. William Watts Hornsby was with the Texas army at San Jacinto when the following raid occurred at his family home near Bastrop.

As I remember what was told to me in regard to the death of Mr's . . . Haggett and Williams, the two Texas Soldiers that were killed by Indians all most in our Grand Father door in the spring of 1836, Santa Anna and his army were raiding in Texas, Murding and destroying evry thing in their path. Rubin Hornsby and a Mr

With a law book in one hand and a rifle in the other, Stephen F. Austin is portrayed as a capable leader in both peace and war (Henry Arthur McArdle, *The Settlement of Austin's Colony* or *The Log Cabin*, oil, 1875, Archives and Information Services Division, Texas State Library, Austin).

Casenors families who lived near them were the only white people that lived in Hornsbys Bend at that time. . . . [T]he Hornsby home was the last house up the Colorado River. . . . Three soldiers were sent up from Bastrop . . . to help guard the Hornsby family. . . .

Two of [the soldiers], Haggett and Williams, proffered to plow a piece of corn the Hornsbys had planted near there house, while the other Soldier, Mr. Cain, and William, Malcom, and two small brothers, Joe and Rubin Jr, were thining oute an other piece father down in the field near the River. They were all unaware that the Indians had quietly crept down on Messrs Haggett and William. . . .

[Back at the Hornsby cabin,] Thomas Hornsby, then a baby of a few yers, came in from play[ing] oute in there yard. [A]llthoug[h] young in years [and] unable to speak very plainly, he knew there was something unusual going on and hastily call[ed], "Daddy come quick! [S]ee a whole ots of men down yonder!"

Mr Hornsby steped oute [on the porch] and at once exclaimed, "Oh, My God! the Indians are killing Haggett and Williams." He at once rushed in [the cabin] to get his own and the Soldiers guns to go to them. The Indians, by this time, had Surrounded there men and were rideing up to . . . each one Shaking hands . . . as they formed a circle arround them.

Mrs Hornsby rushed after her husband, threw her arms arround him, and beged him not to make a useless sacrifice of his own life. . . . [She] pointed oute to him that he could never reach his friends against so many Indians and it was useless for him to try, beging him to stay at the house and protect her and her small children and a daughter. . . .

[Meanwhile,] Miss Casner and Mrs Hornsby hastily arrayed them selves in Mens attire. . . . [B]oth had been taught to shoot there guns all most as well as any of there men folks. . . . Mr. Hornsby rushed oute on the hill side where his boys could see him and rappidly fired his gun to warn them of there danger. There was no chance for [the boys] to reach the house through so many savage Indians. . . . [T]here only escape was to plung into the river which was then Bank full from heavy rains above. They carried over the two small brothers and all secreted them selves in a dense thicket.

Remaining hid oute until after dark, they crossed over the river again and determined to know the fate of there loved ones at the house. William & Malcom left there small brothers in charge of Mr McCain a safe distance away while they cautiously crept up to the house to learn all they could of there people.

After a time and no sign of life—nor sound could be heard except the cries of 16teen calves in there pen, . . . they decided all had been murdered. . . . [T]hey crept into there Smoke house, suppyed them selves with meat and meal to do untel they could reach Bastrop.

With sad hearts, they were on there way back to there friend and little brothers when they decided to trow a rock on there house to arrouse who ever might be in there. . . . To there joy they reccognized there Mothers voice. Instantly they gave the signal for ther friend and the small boys to come in. And, notwithstanding there friends were murdered all most at there door, it was a happy meeting. . . . [T]hey rejoiced that it was not as they had feared. . . . Miss Casnor laughingly told the boys how quickly She and there Mother had doned there cloths and . . . march[ed] in the yard. . . . She said the Indians thought they were men and did not come to the house.

Mr Hornsby & Miss Casner walked oute where they might see Indians if any were still arround. . . . [They] stood guard for Mrs Hornsby while she, with her gun in one hand and sheets and other things necessarry, walked down to where there friends lay dead. . . . [She] straightened them oute as best she could—closeing there eyes and mouths & hopeing the white sheets spread over there lifeless boddies would protect them from the numerous wild anamels until morning [when] they could get help to bring them to the house . . . [and] dig there graves.

These were the first grave made at the Hornsby cemetery and they were burried in a few feete from where they wer killed. They were Single men. If they had any relatives in Texas, it was not known and very little was ever know of there history. One of them came from Alabama and the other I think was from Tennessee. There graves were once paled in. . . . But time has removed these marks and large rocks . . . now . . . mark there graves.

Reprinted with permission from the Hornsby Papers, Texas State Library, courtesy of Reuben Hornsby descendant, Lois Douglas.

Unit Three

THE BLEEDING FRONTIER

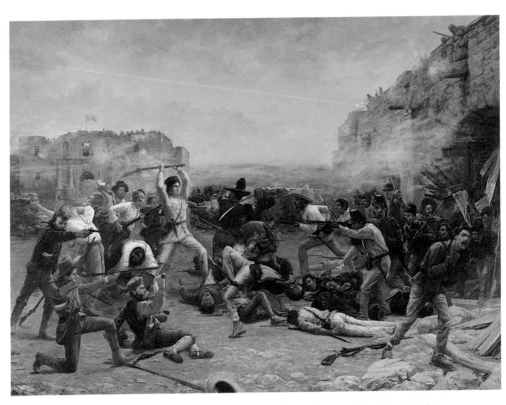

During the final siege of the Alamo, Davy Crockett and 182 others fought valiantly for their lives (Robert Jenkins Onderdonk, *The Fall of the Alamo* or *Crockett's Last Stand*, oil, 1903, Friends of the Governor's Mansion, Austin).

Chapter 9
VICTORY OR DEATH!

Blood of heroes hath stained me:
Let the stones of the Alamo speak
that their immolation
be not
forgotten.

—Part of San Antonio de Valero Mission, The Alamo. This tablet was placed by the Daughters of the Republic of Texas in commemoration of the one-hundredth anniversary of the fall of the Alamo.

By 9:00 a.m., it was all over. The Alamo had fallen. For thirteen days, 183 Texan defenders had held the stone fortress against a constant cannonade and 4,000 Mexican troops. In the predawn grayness of March 6, 1836, the Texans awoke to the sound of a Mexican bugle playing the haunting tune, Degüello. The final assault began. Mexican soldiers poured over the Alamo walls and entered its courtyard. The Texans fought valiantly for their lives but in vain. Every Alamo man was killed.

Santa Anna may have won that battle, but he certainly lost the war. "Victory will cost the enemy so dear, that it will be worse for him than defeat," Colonel William Barrett Travis, the commander of the Alamo, had predicted, three days before he rushed to the north wall of the Alamo to meet his own death.

The following letter, written by Colonel Travis, inflamed passions worldwide. Volunteers rushed to Texas to join the fight, but the Texas Revolution was over before they had even crossed the Sabine River. Many of these Americans liked what they saw when they got there and decided to stick around. They wanted to be part of the noble adventure called Texas, a country born of the blood of heroes such as William Barrett Travis, Commander of the Alamo.

Commandancy of the Alamo—

Bexar, Fby. 24th 1836 —

To the People of Texas & all Americans <u>in the world</u>—

Fellow citizens & compatriots—I am besieged by a thousand or more of the Mexicans under Santa Anna—I have sustained a continual Bombardment & cannonade for 24 hours & have not lost a man—The enemy has demanded a surrender at discretion otherside, the garrison are to be put to the sword, if the fort is taken—I have answered the demand with a cannon shot, & our flag still waves proudly from the walls—<u>I shall never surrender or retreat. Then,</u> I call on you in the name of Liberty, of patriotism & of everything dear to the American character, to come to our aid, with all dispatch—The enemy is receiving reinforcements daily & will no doubt increase to three or four thousand in four or five days. If this call is neglected, I am determined to sustain myself as long as possible & die like a soldier who never forgets what is due to his own honor & that of his country—<u>Victory or Death.</u>

William Barrett Travis
Lt. Col. Comdr.

P.S. The Lord is on our side—when the enemy appeared in sight we had not three bushels of corn—we have since found in deserted houses 80 or 90 bushels & got into the walls 20 or 30 head of Beeves—

Travis

From A Texas Scrapbook: Made Up of the History, Biography, and Miscellany of Texas and Its People, Texas State Historical Association, 1991. Reprinted courtesy Texas State Historical Association, Austin.

Chapter 10
THE RUNAWAY SCRAPE

Texans were horrified to hear the double bad news—not only had the Alamo fallen but the Mexican Army was on the move again. Scouts galloped from settlement to settlement shouting, "The Mexicans are coming! The Mexicans are coming!" And, indeed, they were. General Santa Anna had ordered his thousands of soldiers to sweep across Texas to the Sabine River, burning every town, plantation, farm, and dwelling in their path. Santa Anna was not leaving for Mexico until he was sure he had crushed the Texas rebellion once, and for all.

Texans panicked and deserted their homes. This mass exodus is known as the "Runaway Scrape." Noah Smithwick was one of the last people to leave Bastrop. As he made his way east just ahead of the Mexican army, he noted the desolation of the countryside:

Houses were standing open, the beds unmade, the breakfast things still on the tables, pans of milk moulding in the dairies. There were cribs full of corn, smoke houses full of bacon, yards full of chickens that ran after us for food, nests of eggs in every fence corner . . . cattle cropping the luxuriant grass, hogs, fat and lazy, wallowing in the mud, all abandoned. Forlorn dogs roamed. . . . Hungry cats ran mewing to meet us, rubbing their sides against our legs in token of welcome.

Although in terrible pain from a shattered ankle, General Sam Houston is shown graciously offering Santa Anna a seat following the Battle of San Jacinto (William Henry Huddle, *The Surrender of Santa Anna*, oil, 1886. Archives and Information Services Division, Texas State Library, Austin, Texas).

Dilue Rose Harris was ten years old that spring of 1836 when her family fled its Houston-area farm and joined the flight of the Texas refugees to the U.S. border. In her reminiscences, Dilue describes the Runaway Scrape and her visit to the San Jacinto battlefield.

We left home at sunset, hauling clothes, bedding, and provisions on the sleigh with one yoke of oxen. Mother and I were walking, she with an infant in her arms. Brother drove the oxen, and my two little sisters rode in the sleigh. We were going ten miles to where we could be transferred to Mr. Bundick's cart. Father was helping with the cattle, but he joined us after dark and brought a horse and saddle for brother. . . .

We camped the first night near Harrisburg. . . . Next day we crossed Vince's Bridge and arrived at the San Jacinto in the night. There were fully five thousand people at the [Lynchburg] ferry. The planters from Brazoria and Columbia with their slaves were crossing. We waited for three days before we crossed. . . . Our party consisted of five white families: father's, Mr. Dyer's, Mr. Bell's, Mr. Neal's, and Mr. Bundick's. Father and Mr. Bundick were the only white men in the party, the others being in the army. There were twenty or thirty negroes from Stafford's plantation. . . . Altogether, black and white, there were about fifty of us. Every one was trying to cross first, and it was almost a riot.

We got over the third day, and . . . came to a big prairie. . . . [S]ome of our party wanted to camp; but others said that the

Trinity River was rising, and if we delayed we might not get across. So we hurried on. . . .

Our hardships began at the Trinity. The river was rising and there was a struggle to see who should cross first. Measles, sore eyes, whooping cough, and every other disease that man, woman, or child is heir to, broke out among us. . . . The horrors of crossing the Trinity are beyond my power to describe. One of my little sisters was very sick, and the ferryman said that those families that had sick children should cross first. When our party got to the boat the water broke over the banks above where we were and ran around us. We were several hours surrounded by water. Our family was the last to get to the boat. We left more than five hundred people on the west bank. Driftwood covered the water as far as we could see. The sick child was in convulsions. It required eight men to manage the boat.

When we landed the lowlands were under water, and everybody was rushing for the prairie. Father had a good horse, and Mrs. Dyer let mother have her horse and saddle. Father carried the sick child, and sister and I rode behind mother. She carried father's gun and the little babe. All we carried with us was what clothes we were wearing at the time. The night was very dark. We crossed a bridge that was under water. As soon as we crossed, a man with a cart and oxen drove on the bridge, and it broke down, drowning the oxen. . . .

Father and mother hurried on, and we got to the prairie and found a great many families camped there. A Mrs. Foster invited mother to her camp, and furnished us with supper, a bed, and dry clothes. . . .

The man whose oxen were drowned sold his cart to father for ten dollars. He said that he had seen enough of Mexico and would go back to old Ireland.

It had been five days since we crossed the Trinity, and we had heard no news from the army. The town of Liberty was three miles from where we camped. The people there had not left their homes, and they gave us all the help in their power. My little sister that had been sick died and was buried in the cemetery at Liberty. . . .

We had been at Liberty for three weeks. A Mr. Martin let father use his house. . . . One Thursday evening all of a sudden we heard a sound like distant thunder . . . father said it was cannon, and that the Texans and Mexicans were fighting. He had been through the war of 1812, and knew it was a battle. The cannonading lasted only a few minutes, and father said that the Texans must have been defeated, or the cannon would not have ceased firing so quickly. We left Liberty in half an hour. . . .

We traveled nearly all night, sister and I on horseback and mother in the cart. Father had two yoke of oxen now. . . . We were as wretched as we could be; for we had been five weeks from home, and there was not much prospect of our ever returning. We had not heard a word from brother or the other boys driving the cattle. Mother was sick, and we had buried our dear little sister at Liberty. . . .

We continued our journey through mud and water and . . . we camped. . . .

Then we heard some one calling in the direction of Liberty. We could see a man on horseback waving his hat; and, as we knew there was no one left at Liberty, we thought the Mexican army had crossed the Trinity. . . . [W]hen the riders got near enough for us to understand what he said, it was "Turn back! The Texas army has whipped the Mexican army and the Mexican army are prisoners. No danger! No danger! Turn back!" When he got to the camp he could scarcely speak he was so excited and out of breath. . . .

Father asked the man for an explanation, and he showed a dispatch from General Houston giving an account of the battle and saying it would be safe for people to return to their homes. . . . He said that General Houston was wounded, and that General Santa Anna had not been captured.

The good news was cheering indeed. . . .

We were on the move early the next morning. . . . We crossed the river in a flat boat. . . .

[W]e had a disagreeable time crossing the [Trinity] bay. . . . There was a bayou to cross over which there was no bridge, and the only way to pass was to go three miles through the bay to get around the mouth of the bayou. There were guide-posts to point out the way, but it was very dangerous. If we got near the mouth of the bayou there was quicksand. If the wind rose the waves rolled high.

The bayou was infested with alligators. A few days before our family arrived at the bay a Mr. King was caught by one and carried under water. He was going east with his family. He swam his horses across the mouth of the bayou, and then he swam back to the west side and drove the cart into the bay. His wife and children became frightened, and he turned back and said he would go up the river and wait for the water to subside. He got his family back on land and swam the bayou to bring back the horses.

He had gotten nearly across with them, when a large alligator appeared. Mrs. King first saw it above water and screamed. The alligator struck her husband with its tail and he went under water. There were several men present, and they fired their guns at the animal, but it did no good. It was not in their power to rescue Mr. King. The men waited several days and then killed a beef, put a quarter on the bank, fastened it with a chain, and then watched it until the alligator came out, when they shot and killed it. . . .

We passed the bayou without any trouble . . . except the loss of my sunbonnet. It blew off as we reached the shore. The current was very swift at the mouth of the bayou. Father wanted to swim in and get it for me, but mother begged him not to go in the water, so I had the pleasure of seeing it float away. . . . We saw the big dead alligator, and we were glad to leave the Trinity. . . .

We arrived at Lynchburg in the night. . . . There we met several families that we knew. . . .

We crossed the San Jacinto the next morning and stayed until late in the evening on the battle field. Both armies were camped near. General Santa Anna had been captured. There was great rejoicing at the meeting of friends. Mr. Leo Roark was in the battle. . . . He came to the ferry just as we landed, and it was like seeing a brother. He asked mother to go with him to the camp to see General Santa Anna and the Mexican prisoners. She would not go, because, as she said, she was not dressed for visiting; but she gave sister and me permission to go to the camp. I had lost my bonnet crossing Trinity Bay and was compelled to wear a table cloth again. It was six weeks since we had left home, and our clothes were very much dilapidated. I could not go to see the Mexican prisoners with a table cloth tied on my head for I knew several of the young men. I was on the battle field of San Jacinto the 26th of April, 1836. The 28th was the anniversary of my birth. I was eleven years old. . . .

We visited the graves of the Texans that were killed in the battle, but there were none of them that I knew. The dead Mexicans were lying around in every direction. . . .

We left the battle field in the evening. We had to pass among the dead Mexicans, and father pulled one out of the road, so we could get by without driving over the body, since we could not go around it. The prairie was very boggy, it was getting dark, and there were now twenty or thirty families with us. We were glad to leave the battle field, for it was a gruesome sight. We camped that night on the prairie, and could hear the wolves howl and bark as they devoured the dead.

"*The Reminiscences of Mrs. Dilue Rose Harris*" Quarterly of the Texas State Historical Association, *vol. iv (1900), 85-127, 155-189; vii (1904), 214-222. Reprinted in* Texas Tears and Sunshine: Voices of Frontier Women, *Jo Ella Powell Exley, (ed.) Texas A&M Press, 1985. Reprinted courtesy of Texas A&M Press.*

Famous short story writer, O. Henry, made this engraving, yet signed it "T. J. Owen," a pseudonym (T. J. Owen, *The Battle of Plum Creek*, engraving, 1888, Prints and Photographs Collection, CN 04602, The Center for American History, University of Texas at Austin).

Chapter 11
THE BATTLE OF PLUM CREEK

Early on the morning of August 8, 1840, a perfect cloud of dust appeared below the horizon just west of Linnville, a seaport town on Lavaca Bay, Texas. The few early-risers who witnessed this sight dismissed it as a harmless caballada of horses being brought in from Mexico to trade.

But that was not the case. As those spectators looked on in horror, one thousand war-whooping Comanches rose up atop those very horses galloping toward the sleeping village. They were Penateka warriors and they wanted blood—blood to avenge the deaths of their twelve chiefs in San Antonio the previous spring. When they finished with Linnville—slaughterings its cows, plundering its warehouses, stealing its horses, and, finally, burning it to the ground—the town ceased to exist.

But their "victory" was undone by their greed. Swollen with tons of stolen goods, three thousand equally ill-gotten horses and mules, and several captives, the Comanche warriors left the Gulf Coast and trudged toward home. They decided to take the short-cut across the plains. Their horses and mules were too heavily laden to survive a long journey to the Comanchería, they reasoned, knowing fully well they were vulnerable to ambush returning the way they had come. But they were eager to return to camp to show off their new treasures. They had even packed baby alligators to prove they had raided all the way to the coast. It was foolish, they knew, yet they took the shortcut.

Waiting for them along this shortcut was an enraged team of over two hundred Texas rangers, regulars, local militia, Tonkawa allies, and volunteers under the command of General Edward

Burleson. John Holland Jenkins was part of this volunteer force. Here is his recollection of the unusual battle that followed.

At Lynnville, the Indians burned a few houses, killed a few more citizens, and then went on unmolested. They took two captives, Mrs. Crosby and Mrs. Watts, whose husbands were killed in the fight, and started back on their incoming trail. . . .

By this time, the news having been well ventilated here around Bastrop, General Burleson had raised all the men he possibly could and started out, anxious to intercept them at Plum Creek. . . . We rode until midnight, then halted to rest our horses. Very early the next morning we were again on the warpath. . . .

We fell in with the Guadalupe men in the edge of Big Prairie, near Plum Creek, about two miles from where Lockhart now stands. We were now ordered to dismount, lay aside every weight, examine our arms, and make ready for battle. [Gen. Felix] Huston's men had gotten in ahead of the Indians, and were lying in a little mot of timber, when they heard the Indians coming, they being seemingly ignorant of our close proximity to them, for they were singing, whistling, yelling, and indeed making every conceivable noise. . . .

At length, however, we were discovered by the main force of Indians, who immediately formed a line between us and their pack mules, stolen horses, and other plunder, and awaited our attack. . . .

It was a strange spectacle never to be forgotten, the wild, fantastic band as they stood in battle array, or swept around us with all strategy of Indian warfare. Twenty or thirty warriors, mounted upon splendid horses, tried to ride around us . . . firing upon us as they went. . . . Both horses and riders were decorated most profusely, with all of the beauty and horror of their wild taste combined. Red ribbons streamed out from the horses' tails as they swept around us, riding fast, and carrying all manner of stolen goods upon their heads and bodies.

There was a huge warrior, who wore a stovepipe hat, and another who wore a fine pigeon-tailed cloth coat, buttoned up behind. They seemed to have a talent for finding and blending the strangest, most unheard-of ornaments. Some wore on their heads immense buck and buffalo horns. One headdress struck me particularly. It consisted of a large white crane with red eyes.

In this run-around two warriors were killed, and also a fine horse. We were now ordered to reload, mount, and charge. They at once retreated, though a few stood until we were in fifteen steps of them before starting. In the meantime, the same warriors played around us at the right, trying to divide our attention and force, while the main body of Indians retreated, firing as they went. Soon, however, they struck a very boggy bayou, into which all of their pack mules and horses bogged down. . . . The mules were . . . loaded with all manner of goods, some even carrying hoop-irons to make arrow spikes. They bogged down so close together that a man could have walked along on their bodies *dry*.

Still the Indians retreated while the whites advanced, though the ranks on both sides were constantly growing thinner, for at every thicket a savage left his horse and took to the brush. . . . About twenty warriors kept up their play upon our right, while an equal number of our men kept them at bay. In this side play, Hutch Reid (Hutchinson Reed) was wounded. He undertook to run up on an Indian and shoot him. As he passed, his gun snapped, and before he could check his horse, an arrow struck him just under the shoulder blade, piercing his lungs and lodging against his breast bone. . . .

While halting to rest our horses, we heard a child cry, and upon going into the thicket, a Mr. Carter found a fine Indian baby, which had been left in the retreat.

Joe Hornsby and I were riding about two hundred yards in front of Burlesons' main army, watching for Indian signs and trails as we went. Suddenly we came in sight of about thirty Indians some distance ahead. . . . I galloped back to notify Burleson . . . we cut in ahead of them and advanced upon them. In thirty steps of them, Burleson ordered us to fire. . . . At one time here, I felt as if my "time" had come, sure enough. We had fired one round, and I was down loading my gun when I saw an Indian approaching me with gun presented. At this critical moment Joe Burleson shot, killing him instantly. We discovered afterward that the Indian's gun was not loaded, and he was playing a "bluff." . . .

We had a hot race after another warrior on foot, who was unarmed except bow and arrow. . . . The hardy warrior made a brave . . . fight. . . . I killed him just in time to save myself.

What fancies they had in the way of ornamenting themselves! This savage presented a strange picture as he lay decked in beads, etc., sleeping the "dreamless sleep" of death. He also carried around his neck a tiny whistle and tin trumpet.

The stolen horses, mules, and goods were divided among the soldiers . . . . A Comanche mule fell to my lot, and an odd specimen he was, with red ribbons on ears and tail. . . .

We also found the body of Mrs. Crosby, whom they had killed when obliged to retreat, and nearby we found Mrs. Watts, whom they had also left for dead, having shot an arrow into her breast. A thick corset board had received and impeded its force, so that though wounded, she was still alive. She was a remarkably fine looking woman, but was sunburned almost to a blister.

Recollections of Early Texas: The Memoirs of John Holland Jenkins, *ed. by John Holmes Jenkins III. Copyright © 1958. Reprinted by permission of the University of Texas Press.*

Chapter 12
THE BLACK BEAN LOTTERY

The day of the drawing (26th) was dark cloudy high winds &
waves of sand flying. No birds to sing no crickets to chirp no
owls to whoop in all this land nor no stock in sight.

> —Big Foot Wallace, in a letter to Nora Franklin, 1888
> *Wallace (William Alexander Anderson) Papers, The Center for American History,*
> *The University of Texas at Austin.*

*Seeking revenge for a brief Mexican occupation of San Antonio
in the fall of 1842, an unauthorized force of bold Texans marched
on Mexico later that year. They arrived at Mier, a dusty adobe town
in the Northern Mexico desert, and were immediately surrounded
by a large Mexican force. The Texans fought fiercely, but finding
themselves outnumbered ten-to-one, they decided to surrender.
They laid down their arms, believing they would be treated as prisoners of war under Mexican terms and held near the border.*

*Instead, the Texas prisoners were lined up and told to march to
Mexico City. One hundred miles north of Salado, Texas Ranger
Captain Ewen Cameron and several others decided to make a
break for it. They overpowered their Mexican guards and escaped
into the Sierra Nevada Mountains.*

*For seven days, the fugitives wandered in circles, looking for the
Río Grande. They became separated and quickly lost their way. It
was the dry season; their mouths grew parched with thirst. They
dug wildly for wet earth to soothe their swollen tongues. A few lost
their minds and drank their own urine, dying a dreadful death. The
Mexican soldiers had no trouble rounding up all but a few.*

*William A. A. "Big Foot" Wallace, one of the Texas prisoners,
was a Scotsman who had come to Texas to avenge a relative's*

Frederic Remington admired the people who settled the West. In this scene, Texas prisoners of war stand under the hot noonday sun, nobly awaiting their fate (Frederic Remington, *The Mier Expedition: Drawing of the Black Bean*, oil, 1896, The Museum of Fine Arts, Houston; (43.14) The Hogg Brothers Collection, gift of Miss Ima Hogg).

death at the massacre of Goliad. Big Foot was one of the "men with the bark on," a term coined by western artist Frederic Reming-ton to describe the rough-and-ready men attracted to Texas. Here is Big Foot Wallace's account of the peculiar sentence imposed by the "Supreme Government of Mexico" on the Texan prisoners-of-war.

After our long sojourn at Saltillo, we were one morning roused up by our guard, and told to get ready to march, as we were to start that day to the City of Mexico. A few moments afterward the guard paraded in front of our quarters. We were taken out and formed into line, and marched off on the road back toward Ran-cho Salado, where some weeks previously, we had risen upon and surprised the guard. . . . Handcuffed and bound together in pairs . . . we were driven along the road at a gait that would have been "killing" even to men that were not fettered as we were.

On the evening of the fourth day . . . we came in sight, once more, of the lonely, desolate Rancho Salado. The officer now in command of the guard, Colonel Ortez, had spoken kindly to us frequently during the day, telling us to "be cheerful and walk up fast, for that the sooner we arrived at the City of Mexico, the sooner we would be liberated and sent back home." Notwith-standing these assurances, from the first moment the men caught sight of the dismal old ranch, whether it was the dreari-ness of the locality, or the recollection of what had happened there when we rose on the guard, and of the sufferings and disas-ters that followed in the wake of that event, or whether it was some dim foreboding of the "bloody scene" that was to be en-acted there again so soon, that weighed upon the minds of the men, I know not; but not a word was uttered by any one, as we trudged along silent and depressed, until we reached the hated spot, and were once more securely fastened up in the same corral we had occupied before.

But a few moments elapsed before an officer, accompanied by an interpreter, entered the corral, and calling our attention, proceeded to read to us from a paper he held in his hand, a mandate from the "Supreme Government of Mexico," ordering the instant execution of every tenth man. Some of the more sanguine among us fully thought that the paper contained an order for our release, and eagerly crowded around the interpreter to hear the joyful news; but when the purport of the writing was explained to us by the interpreter, this barbarous decimation of our number came upon us so unexpectedly that we stood for a moment stunned and confused by the suddenness of the shock. Then a reaction took place, and if our hands had only been unshackled, unarmed as we were, the old Rancho Salado would have witnessed another up-rising, ten times as bloody as the first; but when we looked upon our manacled limbs, and the serried ranks and glittering bayonets of the large guard drawn up around us, we saw at once that any attempt at resistance would be utter folly, and we quietly submitted to our fate.

It was determined that the seventeen men to be executed should be selected by lottery, and in a little while a squad of Mexican officers came into the corral, preceded by a soldier bearing an earthen vessel, which he placed upon a low stone wall bounding the farther side of the corral, and which was intended to hold a number of white and black beans, corresponding to the number of men and officers in our command. The Mexican officers stationed themselves near the earthen pot, to overlook and superintend the lottery, and see that every one had a fair chance for his life. One of them then proceeded to count out so many white beans, which he poured into the vessel, and then dropped in the fatal seventeen black ones on top of them, covering the whole with a thick napkin or cloth. We were then formed into line and drawn up in front of the low wall on which the earthen pot had been placed.

Before the drawing began, they informed us that if any man drew out more than one bean, and either of them should prove a black one, he would be regarded as having drawn a black one solely, and be shot accordingly.

Our commissioned officers were ordered to draw first. Captain Cameron stepped forward, and without the slightest visible trepidation put his hand under the cloth and drew out a white bean. He had observed, when the Mexican officer put the beans in the pot, that he poured the white in first and the black ones on top of them, and then set it down without shaking, possibly with the intention of forcing as large a number as possible of the black beans upon our commissioned officers, who were to have the first drawing. When he returned to his place in the line, he whispered to those nearest him, "Dip deep, boys," and by following his advice all the officers drew white beans except Captain Eastland.

After the officers had all drawn, the "muster-rolls" of the men were produced, and we were called forward as our names appeared upon them. Some of the Mexican officers present were evidently much affected by the courage and nonchalance manifested by the men in this fiery trial; others, on the contrary, seemed to enjoy the whole proceedings hugely, particularly one little swarthy baboon-visaged chap, that looked as if he had subsisted all his life on a short allowance of red pepper and *cigaritos*. He appeared to take an especial delight in the hesitation of some of the men when they put their hands into the vessel, for even the bravest felt some reluctance to draw when he knew that life or certain death depended upon the color of the bean he might select. Whenever there was the slightest hesitation, this officer would say, in apparently the most commisserating tone: "Take your time, *mi niño* (my child); dont hurry yourself, *mi muchacho* (my boy); be careful, *mi pobrecito* (poor fellow); you know if you get a black bean you will be taken out and shot in ten minutes"—a fact we had already been fully apprised of.

"Ah! that's unfortunate," he would say, when a poor fellow drew a black bean; "but better luck to you the next time."

Yet, all the while he was talking in this way, in the kindest accents, a devilish grin on his baboon-face indicated the great pleasure he took in the anxiety and distress of these "poor fellows."

I am not of a revengeful disposition, but if that Mexican had even fallen into my power, his chances of living to a "good old age" would have been miserably slim. . . . I'll tell you how I would have served him. I would have bought a bushel of black beans, cooked them about half done in a big pot, and made him sit down upon it and eat until he bursted. I'd have given him a dose that would have stretched his little tawny hide as tight as a bass-drum. . . .

Those who drew black beans seemed to care very little about it. Occasionally one would remark, as he drew out the fatal color, "Well, boys, the jig is up with me;" or, "They have taken my sign in at last;" . . . apparently as unconcerned as if he had no interest whatever in what was going on around him.

There was but a single exception to this. One poor fellow, a messmate of mine, too, appeared to be completely overcome by his apprehensions of drawing a black bean. He stood until his own time to draw came round, wringing his hands and moaning audibly, and continually telling those near him that he knew he should draw a black bean. . . . When his turn came, he hung back, and absolutely refused to go up at all until a file of Mexican soldiers forced him forward at the points of their bayonets. He hesitated so long after he put his hand into the vessel containing the beans that a Mexican officer near him pricked him severely with his sword to make him withdraw it. All this, of course, was immensely gratifying to the little baboon-faced official, who *"niñoed"* and *"pobrecitoed"* him in this kindest tones, all the while, though evidently snickering and laughing in his sleeve at the fears exhibited by the *"pobrecito."*

At last the poor fellow was forced to withdraw his hand, and his presentiment proved too true, for in it he held the fatal black bean. He turned deadly pale as his eyes rested upon it, but apparently he soon resigned himself to his inevitable fate, for he never uttered a word of complaint afterward. I pitied him from the bottom of my heart.

My name beginning with W, was, of course, among the last on the roll, and when it came to my turn to draw, so many more white beans than black had been draw out in proportion, that there could have been no great difference in the number of each. I observed twenty-four white beans drawn out in succession. The chances of life and death for me were, therefore, not so very unequal. I will frankly confess, when I put my hand into the pot and this fact recurred to my mind, a spasm of fear or dread sent a momentary chill to my heart, but I mastered it quickly, and before even the lynx-eye of the little baboon-faced official detected any sign of such weakness. At any rate, he bestowed none of his endearing epithets upon me.

All the time the drawing had been going on I stood pretty close to the scene of operations, and I thought I could perceive a slight difference in the size of the black and white beans—that the former were a shade larger than the latter. This difference, I know, may have been purely imaginary, but at any rate, I was eventually decided by it in my choice of a bean.

When I first put my hand in the pot I took up several beans at once in my fingers, and endeavored to distinguish their color by the *touch*, but they all felt precisely alike. I then dropped them and picked up two more, and after fingering them carefully for an instant, I thought that one of them seemed a little larger than the other. I dropped that one like a hot potato, and drew out the one left. It was a white one, of course, or I should not now be here to tell my story—but not a *very* white one, and when I cast my eyes upon it, it looked to me as "black as the ace of spades."

I felt certain for a moment that my fate was sealed, but when I handed it to the Mexican officer who received them as they were drawn out, I saw that he put it on the wall with the white beans, and not into his waistcoat pocket, as he had done the black ones. I knew then that I was safe, and the revulsion of feeling was so great and rapid that I can compare it to nothing except the sudden lifting of an immense weight from off one's shoulders. I felt as light as a feather, though I weighed at least one hundred and seventy pounds. . . .

When the drawing was completed, the white and black beans were carefully counted over again, and the number found to tally with that of the men. Those that had drawn black beans were kept separate from the rest of us, and, in a few moments after the drawing was concluded, they were marched off in two squads, and shortly afterward repeated volleys of musketry were heard, and we knew that their cares and troubles were forever ended in this world.

One of them, however, a man by the name of Shepperd, as we learned subsequently, made a most miraculous escape for the time being. When they were fired upon by the guard, Shepperd fell and pretended to be dead, though, in fact, he was only slightly wounded. He was left on the ground with the dead bodies of his companions, and when night came he got up and went off without being observed. The next morning, when the Mexicans examined the bodies again, they were greatly astonished to find that one was missing, and could not be accounted for satis- factorily in any way. Shepperd wandered around for several weeks without being recaptured, but at length he was discovered, taken back to Saltillo, and shot to death in the public square, and his body carried out and left unburied on the commons.

From The Adventures of Big Foot Wallace, *John C. Duval, J. W. Burke & Co., 1970.*

Unit Four

THE BUFFALO BOWMEN

Over six hundred wigwams made up this Comanche village situated just
north of the Red River. In the foreground is the chief's wigwam (George
Catlin, *Comanche Village, Women Dressing Robes and Drying Meat,* oil on
canvas, 1834, National Museum of American Art, Smithsonian Institution,
gift of Mrs. Joseph Harrison, Jr.).

Chapter 13
A COMANCHE VILLAGE

Three little letters—"G.T.T."— told the whole story. Over a century ago, this code was chalked on doorposts of abandoned houses across the South. The inhabitants had dropped everything and "Gone to Texas." The Texas government was promising every family man at least 640 acres of free land! The rush was on.

The eastern portion of the Republic quickly filled up. Cotton plantations sprouted in the fertile bottomland of the Brazos River Valley. Each new wave of immigrants pushed the frontier further west, into the beautiful and grassy Great Plains region—where the buffalo roamed and so did the mounted Comanche. Years of bloody conflict followed.

Noah Smithwick, an old settler, lived with the Comanches for three months. Here he recalls a conversation with the old Comanche chief, Muguara.

We have set up our lodges in these groves and swung our children from these boughs from time immemorial. When game beats away from us we pull down our lodges and move away, leaving no trace to frighten it, and in a little while it comes back. But the white man comes and cuts down the trees, building houses and fences, and the buffalo get frightened and leave and never come back, and the Indians are left to starve, or, if we follow the game, we trespass on the hunting ground of other tribes and war ensues. . . .

No, the Indians were not made to work. If they build houses and try to live like white men they will all die.

From Evolution of a State, *Noah Smithwick, University of Texas Press, 1983. Reprinted by permission of the University of Texas Press.*

Chapter 14
A TONKAWA FEAST

The Tonkawas were another Plains Indian tribe dependent on the buffalo for food, clothing, and shelter. But the Tonkawas did not limit their diet to jerked buffalo meat. Central Texas had a smorgasbord of good things to eat, including rabbits, fish, deer, birds, rabbits, and turtles as well as nuts, fruits, and berries. Fried rattlesnake was a particular favorite among the Tonkawas. And, on very special occasions, such as triumph in battle, the whole band would come together for a dance and a banquet—to feast on the flesh of their mortal enemies, the Comanches.

Noah Smithwick witnessed one of these bizarre banquets. Here is his tale.

Of the many different tribes inhabiting Texas prior to its occupation by the Anglo-Saxon, only the Karankawas and Tonkawas were known to be cannibals. . . .

The Tonkawas . . . had uniformly manifested a friendly disposition toward the whites, assisting them in their warfare against the hostile tribes, gathering in the scalps and devouring the flesh of the enemy killed in battle, celebrating the victory with a feast and scalp dance. . . .

The only one I ever witnessed was in Webber's prairie, the occasion being the killing of a Comanche, one of a party that had been on a horse stealing trip down into Bastrop. They were hotly

Horses were invaluable to the Plains Indians. When a Tonkawa warrior died, his horse was considered so much a part of him that it was killed, too (Detail from John Mix Stanley, *Ko-rak-koo-kiss, a Tonoccono (Tonkawa) Warrior,* oil, 1844, National Museum of American Art, Smithsonian Institution, Gift of the Misses Henry, 1908).

pursued, and . . . they mounted a warrior on Manlove's big horse, which was part of the booty, and left him behind as rear guard, while the balance hurried the stolen horses away. The Tonkawas joined in the pursuit and when the pursuers came in sight of the lone rear guardsman three of the most expert Tonks were mounted on the three fleetest horses and sent to dispatch him. This they soon accomplished, his steed being a slow one. After killing and scalping him they refused to continue the chase, saying they must return home to celebrate the event, which they accordingly did by a feast and scalp dance.

Having fleeced off the flesh of the dead Comanche, they borrowed a big wash kettle from Puss Webber, into which they put the Comanche meat, together with a lot of corn and potatoes—the most revolting mess my eyes ever rested on. When the stew was sufficiently cooked and cooled to allow of its being ladled out with the hands the whole tribe gathered round, dipping it up with their hands and eating it as greedily as hogs. Having gorged themselves on this delectable feast they lay down and slept till night, when the entertainment was concluded with the scalp dance.

Gotten up in all the hideousness of war paint and best breech-clouts, the warriors gathered round in a ring, each one armed with some ear-torturing instrument, which they operated in unison with a drum made of dried deer skin stretched tightly over a hoop, at the same time keeping up a monotonous "Ha, ah, ha!" raising and lowering their bodies in time that would have delighted a French dancing master, every muscle seeming to twitch in harmony. Meanwhile some old hag of a squaw would present to each in turn an arm or leg of the dead foe, which they would bite at viciously, catching it in their teeth and shaking it like savage dogs. And high over all waved from the point of a lance the scalp, dressed and painted, held aloft by a patriotic squaw. The orgies were kept up till the performers were forced to desist from sheer exhaustion.

From Evolution of a State, Noah Smithwick, University of Texas Press, 1983. Reprinted by permission of the University of Texas Press.

French artist, Théodore Gentilz, frequently walked from Castroville to San Antonio, a distance of twenty-five miles. It was during these walks that he befriended a band of Lipan Apaches (Jean Louis Théodore Gentilz, *Camp of the Lipans*, oil, 1896, Witte Museum, San Antonio).

Chapter 15
LIPAN GROVE

Like the Comanches, the Lipan Apaches were nomadic buffalo hunters, living in tepees and following game. The Lipan Apaches, too, were expert horsemen and bowmen. It was said that a Lipan Apache warrior could shoot twenty arrows before a frontiersman could fire one shot and reload his rifle. Highly mobile, both tribes roamed the plains, terrorizing Spanish missions, white frontier towns, and rival Indian camps.

Competing for the same resource—buffalo—meant continual warfare between these two Plains Indian groups. The Comanches finally won, asserting their control over the Texas Plains by pushing the Apaches farther and farther south and west.

In a strange twist of history, several Lipan Apaches retaliated by joining forces with their former enemies, the white settlers, and forming a mutual defense against the indomitable Comanches.

Julia Lee Sinks was not yet twenty years old when she came to Austin from Cincinnati in 1840. By this time, it was commonplace to see Indians walking the streets of the Capital of the Republic. Nevertheless, it still made Julia uneasy. In this passage from her memoirs, "Early Days in Texas," Julia recounts her visit to a Lipan Apache camp in Austin and her encounters with Flacco, a respected Lipan Apache chief.

The Lipans [Lipan Apaches] . . . had made a treaty of peace, and from among them the whites had found some excellent spies. But upon the whole, friendly as they pretended to be, there were very few who could be risked at a safe distance from discovery. I well remember one bright afternoon in the summer of 1840 visiting with others a camp of Lipans. It was situated on a small knoll back of where the present capitol stands, overshadowed by a few straggling trees. . . . [I]t was . . . known . . . as Lipan Grove.

On the grassy level between, the Indian women were herding their horses, and their tinkling bells sounded in sweet unison with the beautiful scene. The smoke of the campfire on the knoll curled up among the scanty branches of the trees. By the fire sat two aged Indians, a man and a woman, roasting and eating rawhide, with more appearance of conjugal enjoyment than is often witnessed among the red tribes. . . .

On the plain below, some distance away, a group of young horsemen were trying the speed of their horses, their spirited motions giving the only section to the otherwise quiet scene. . . .

[A]s we advanced to the camp we were met by a tall, brawny white man, habited as an Indian. He came forward with a familiar "howdy" in real Indian style—that is, when they have an end in view. He had smeared his cheeks with dark grease, and while speaking to us he stood scratching it with his finger nails into Egyptian water lines over his brazen cheeks.

When one of the company said with surprise, "He surely is an American," he turned to a young Indian who was seated on the ground combing his hair with a fine comb . . . and said some words, among which was easily distinguished "Americano," showing he clearly understood us, and at which the young Indian laughed. How I pityingly wondered what unfortunate mother had produced such a renegade son.

He pulled up a buffalo skin, and, bowing beside it, waved us to it for a seat. We declined the hospitality. It was the nearest approach to entire savagery with which we had ever come in contact.

I think the treaty of peace had not long been made with them. We knew that individuals had acted as spies against the Comanches with much success, but still I could not look in their savage faces and feel that they were friends. . . .

But out of this tribe, though said to be a Comanche adopted into it in childhood, came the truest friend that Texas ever had among the red men. . . . [T]his . . . fellow, well known to the inhabitants of Austin, had in him the stamp of true nobleness. He attached himself so strongly to Captain Mark B. Lewis that he was like his shadow. In reclaiming the forty horses from the Indians . . . by Captain Lewis, Flacco was one of the foremost.

In the battle of Red Fork . . . he was one of the spies who took him in a bee line fifteen miles to the Comanche camp. And in the battle of the San Saba . . . he was again among them fighting like a white man. Upon the return of the army from the Rio Grande, in 1842, he was left in charge of the extra horses, several hundred in number, by General Somerville, and lost his life in the undertaking by other Indians, or, as many thought, by some renegade white men in the army. . . .

I well remember the first time and the last time I ever spoke to this anomaly [Flacco]. The first time was at a party in the senate chamber of the old capitol. . . . Flacco, following in the wake of Captain Lewis, offered his hand to whomsoever the captain greeted. I touched it with fear, mingled with feelings near akin to repugnance . . . though it was offered with such a smiling face. . . . The last time I spoke to the grand savage, Vasquez had entered San Antonio in the early spring of 1842 and an alarm had seized the inhabitants of Austin. It was known that armies had passed through the interior of Texas. . . . Fears were entertained that the town would be invaded, and the excitement . . . was seen in all directions. . . .

Passing down the avenue where the people with few exceptions were making preparations to find places of safety we saw Flacco sitting on the gallery of a small house, known as the "Moreland house," connected with the land office, apparently absorbed in thought. The commotion that filled the town seemed in strong contrast to the silent Indian, who sat like a brooding spirit mourning our fallen prosperity. He was wrapped in an immense scarlet blanket, with his long black hair parted in the middle and covering his shoulders.

As we approached he rose from his chair, and, holding his blanket with the grace of a Roman about his tall person, he executed two proud salaams, one for myself and one for my companion without uttering a word, and then quietly seated himself again. He had not then received the compliment that President Houston afterward bestowed upon him.

When [Houston] invited Castro, the chief of the Lipans, to the city of Houston to meet him in council, he gracefully added, with his compliments, for Colonel Flacco to come also. . . . It was after this, when he [Flacco] passed through La Grange on his way to Houston, that the autograph . . . was obtained from him. . . . I suppose it is the last thing in existence that ever belonged to him, and it has been preserved ever since 1842 by the writer as a memento of the past.

Sinks (Julia Lee) Papers, The Center for American History, The University of Texas at Austin.

Unit Five
THE DAILY RHYTHMS

There was never a dull moment in Main Plaza, the hub of San Antonio life in the 1840s (William Samuel, *West Side Main Plaza*, oil, 1849, Witte Museum, San Antonio).

Chapter 16
THE STREET LIFE OF
OLD SAN ANTONE

San Antonio was already more than a century old when Texas became a republic in 1836. Established in 1718, it served as a Spanish outpost midway between the missions in East Texas and Spanish settlements in northern Mexico. Over time, a road developed from the San Juan Bautista mission near Eagle Pass through San Antonio and on to Nacogdoches. It was called the "King's Highway," or El Camino Real. This became the major supply route from Mexico into Texas and was what transformed San Antonio into the largest settlement in Spanish Texas.

San Antonio was still the most populous city in Texas when Frederick Law Olmsted visited there in 1854. In his journal, Frederick likened the seductive mystique of San Antonio to that of another very old American city, New Orleans. Here are his impressions.

The street-life of San Antonio is more varied than might be supposed. Hardly a day passes without some noise. If there be no personal affray to arouse talk, there is some Government train to be seen, with its hundred of mules, on its way from the coast to a fort above; or a Mexican ox-train from the coast, with an interesting supply of ice, or flour, or matches, or of whatever the shops find themselves short. A Government express clatters off, or news arrives from some exposed outpost, or from New Mexico.

An Indian in his finery appears on a shaggy horse, in search of blankets, powder, and ball. Or at the least, a stagecoach with the "States" or the Austin mail rolls into the plaza and discharges its load of passengers and newspapers.

The street affrays are numerous and characteristic. I have seen, for a year or more, a San Antonio weekly, and hardly a number fails to have its fight or its murder. More often than otherwise, the parties meet upon the plaza by chance, and each, on catching sight of his enemy, draws a revolver, and fires away. As the actors are under more or less excitement, their aim is not apt to be of the most careful and sure, consequently it is, not seldom, the passers-by who suffer. Sometimes it is a young man at a quiet dinner in a restaurant, who receives a ball in the head; sometimes an old negro woman, returning from market, who gets winged. After disposing of all their lead, the parties close, to try their steel, but as this species of metallic amusement is less popular, they generally contrive to be separated ("Hold me! Hold me!") by friends before the wounds are mortal. If neither is seriously injured, they are brought to drink together on the following day, and the town waits for the next excitement. . . . Murders . . . are common here.

The town amusements of a less exciting character are not many. There is a permanent company of Mexican mountebanks, who give performances . . . two or three times a week, parading, before night, in their spangled tights with drum and trombone through the principal streets. They draw a crowd . . . and this attracts a few sellers of whisky, *tortillas,* and *tamaules* (corn slap-jacks and hashed meat in corn-shucks), all by the light of torches making a ruddily picturesque evening group.

From A Journey Through Texas Or, A Saddle-Trip on the Southwestern Frontier, *Frederick Law Olmsted, pp. 158-159, 1989. By permission of the University of Texas Press.*

Chapter 17
FRONTIER CUISINE

On his 1854 saddle-trip through Texas, New Yorker Frederick Law Olmsted found "sunny beauty of scenery and luxuriance of soil." Olmsted had no problem finding great landscapes; what he could not find was a good meal. In almost every settlement he visited, he was served the same "three articles"—jerked meat ("fry"), cornbread ("pone"), and coffee.

Yet Olmsted did not give up hope. Traveling abroad had taught him to look for creature comforts in capital cities. Even though a norther had just plunged Central Texas into a deep freeze, Olmsted set out on horseback for the Texas capital, Austin.

He and his younger brother, John Hull, their two mounts, and their pack mule, "Mr. Brown," rode for two days until they reached Bastrop, where they planned to cross the Colorado River to Austin. It was dusk by then, yet they did not make camp for the night. Rather, they pushed on toward the ferry crossing. The road grew indistinct in the fading twilight, and the brothers were forced to follow wagon tracks in the dark. The ferry man was alarmed when they thumped on his door at nine o'clock that night. He felt sure someone must be sick, it was so extraordinary for anyone to want to cross the river at that late hour.

Frederick Olmsted did reach Austin, but the meal of his dreams stayed way out of reach. It teased him a little while longer. Good food was in his future, but it lay down the trail a piece. It was going to pop up and surprise him when he least expected it.

In the following excerpt from his book, A Journey Through Texas, Frederick Olmsted describes two very different Texas towns, Austin and Castroville.

Founder Henri Castro patterned Castroville after European villages in which small town lots were surrounded by farmland (Rúdolph Mueller, *Mother House of the Sisters of Divine Providence and Vicinity, Castroville, Texas*, oil, ca. 1873, Witte Museum, San Antonio).

AUSTIN

We had reckoned upon getting some change of diet when we reached the capital of the state, and upon having good materials not utterly spoiled, by carelessness, ignorance, or nastiness, in cooking. We reckoned without our host.

We arrived in a norther, and were shown, at the hotel to which we had been recommended, into an exceedingly dirty room, in which two of us slept with another gentleman, who informed us that it was the best room in the house. The outside door, opening upon the ground, had no latch, and during the night it was blown open by the norther, and after we had made two ineffectual attempts to barricade it, was kept open till morning.

Before daylight, a boy came in and threw down an armful of wood by the fire-place. He appeared again, an hour or two afterwards, and made a fire. When the breakfast-bell rung, we all turned out in haste, though our boots were gone and there was no water. At this moment, as we were reluctantly pulling on our clothing, a negro woman burst into the room, leaving the door open, and laid a towel on the wash-table. "Here!" we cried, as she ran to the door again; "bring us some water, and have our boots brought back." She stood half outside the door, and shaking her finger at us in a weird manner, replied: "Haant got no time, master—got fires to make and every ting"; and she vanished.

When finally we got to breakfast, and had offered us—but I will not again mention the three articles—only the "fry" had been changed for the worse before it was fried—we naturally began to talk of changing our quarters and trying another of the hotels. Then up spoke a dark, sad man at our side—"You can't do better than stay here; I have tried both the others, and I came here yesterday because the one I was at was *too dirty!*" And the man said this, with that leopard-skin pattern of a tablecloth, before him, with those grimy tools in his hands, and with the hostler in his frock, smelling strongly of the stable. . . . Never did we see any wholesome food on that table. It was a succession of burnt flesh of swine and bulls, decaying vegetables, and sour and mouldy farinaceous glues, all pervaded with rancid butter. . . .

After spending a pleasant week in Austin, we crossed the Colorado, into, distinctively, Western Texas. . . .

[T]he route to San Antonio lay through a country very similar to that over which we were now passing, with occasional belts of post-oak, and now and then, a piece of broad river bottom. . . .

We saw some large herds in the finest condition, and it seemed to us the richest grazing district for cattle or sheep we had yet traversed. As we got nearer San Antonio, we passed a greater number of Mexican ranches than we had before seen. Two of them we had occasion to enter. One was a double cabin, in American style. A man in red sash and drawers lay upon the bed, which was almost the only piece of furniture, tossing and playing with a child. We inquired if we could purchase any meat. He referred us to his wife, who was in the garden behind. Passing through, we found the lady, who took down for us about two yards of meat, from several hundred which were drying on a clothes-line. It was cut in strips an inch thick, and was quite hard and dark-colored. Paying at the rate of a dime a yard, we carried it to camp, but found it so tough and so far tainted as to be quite useless. . . .

The year was now well advanced; summer clothing was already sported in San Antonio, and the markets were abundantly supplied with vegetables from the new-made gardens. . . .

We rode before evening to the Medina, twenty-five miles. Imagine, for the country, a rolling sheet of the finest grass, sprinkled thick with bright, many-hued flowers, with here and there a live-oak, and an occasional patch of mesquit trees, which might be pictured as old neglected peach-orchards. . . . Northward, the hills . . . swell gradually higher, until they end in a blue and mountainous line. . . .

The country is almost unoccupied. There are one or two little settlements of Mexicans and Germans along the road, owners of the few cattle that luxuriate in this superb pasture. Their houses are *jacals,* of sticks and mud, with a thick projecting thatch. . . .

The Medina [River] is the very ideal of purity. The road crosses upon white limestone rocks, which give a peculiar brilliancy to its emerald waters. It runs knee deep, and twenty or thirty yards wide, with a rapid descent.

CASTROVILLE

Upon its [the Medina's] bank stands Castroville—a village containing a colony of Alsatians, who are proud here to call themselves Germans, but who speak French, or a mixture of French and German. The cottages are scattered prettily, and there are two churches—the whole aspect being as far from Texan as possible. It might sit for the portrait of one of the poorer villages of the upper Rhone valley. Perhaps the most remarkable thing is the hotel, by M. Tardé, a two-story house, with double galleries, and the best inn we saw in the state. How delighted and astonished many a traveler must have been, on arriving from the plains at this first village, to find not only his dreams of white bread, sweetmeats and potatoes realized, but napkins, silver forks, and radishes, French servants, French neatness, French furniture, delicious French beds, and the *Courrier des Etats Unis*; and more, the lively and entertaining bourgeoise.

From A Journey Through Texas Or, A Saddle-Trip on the Southwestern Frontier, *Frederick Law Olmsted, pp. 111-112; 276-277, 1989. By permission of the University of Texas Press.*

In this pleasant domestic scene, a calf tenderly nuzzles Marie Petri, the artist's sister (Friedrich Richard Petri, *The Pioneer Cowpen*, watercolor, 1853, Texas Memorial Museum, Courtesy Russell Fish, III).

Chapter 18
WOMAN'S WORK

Man may work from sun to sun
But woman's work is never done.

—Old Saying

*Without the help of the women, Texas could not have been set-
tled. The men grabbed the headlines—Sam Houston's army de-
feating the Mexicans at San Jacinto, Jack Hays' Texas Rangers
chasing off the Comanches, Colonel William B. Travis' looking
death in the eye at the Alamo. Undoubtedly, it was the men who
found the land and secured it. But it was the women who came
later who made the settlement home. Their behind-the-scenes con-
tribution was, perhaps, somewhat less glamorous than the men's.
But it was just as important. For it was the women who gave
Texas its roots.*

*On the frontier, there was no rest for women. Many died in child-
birth. Cholera and yellow fever took away their precious children.
A Mexican invasion or Indian attack was a constant worry. Life
grew lonely so far away from loved ones back east.*

*And, of course, there were the chores. Mathilda Doebbler Gruen
Wagner was a German immigrant who settled near Fredericksburg
in the mid-1800s. Here she recounts her average day on the farm.*

This was a little of my day. When you first get up in the morning, before daybreak, you start your fire in the wood stove or the chimney and put your coffee on. Then, just as it is getting light over the hills, you go after the calves. When you bring back the calves, you milk the cows; then bring the calves to their mother cows.

Leaving them for a while, you fix breakfast, which is a big meal. After breakfast, at a time when people are getting up in the cities nowadays, you skim the milk and make the butter, feed the dogs, cats, and the hogs the clabber, and turn the calves in to their pasture and the cows in theirs.

When the butter is made and the dishes washed, the house spic and span, you go to help in the fields. The woman leaves the little baby at the edge of the field with a quilt put above it so the sun won't harm it. When the baby cries the woman leaves the hoe or plow or her work in the field and goes to tend it or nurse it. There was usually a little baby or several small children at a time.

When the sun is in the middle of the sky it is time for dinner. The woman leaves for the house and prepares the food. After eating, the men might lay down for a little while to rest, but there is no rest for the women.

There is always work to be done. In the afternoon there may be more work in the fields, or baking, candlemaking, soap-making, sewing, mending, any of the hundred pressing tasks, and then the calves must again be rounded up and brought home as the shadows fall, the cows milked, the chickens fed, always something, early and late.

I Think Back: Being the Memoirs of Grandma Gruen. San Antonio, privately printed, 1937. Reprinted in Texas Tears and Sunshine: Voices of Frontier Women, Jo Ella Powell Exley, Texas A&M Press, 1985. Reprinted courtesy of Texas A&M University Press.

Chapter 19
HOME ALONE

Texas is a heaven for men and dogs,
but a hell for women and oxen.

—Old Saying

When their menfolk said, "Load up the wagon! Round up the children and the animals! We're going to Texas!," immigrant women dutifully left behind all they held dear—their homes and gardens, their friends and sisters and mothers, their churches—to travel to a land they had never even seen.

They found Texas to be a beautiful yet frightening place. Most families settled in log cabins out in the middle of nowhere, miles from the nearest neighbor. Out of necessity, the men were gone for long stretches of time to hunt game, battle Indians, visit the seat of government, or to check on cattle. The women were expected to stay home—alone—and hold down the fort. It was lonely and scary.

Many women coped with the enforced solitude by writing. They kept scrupulous diaries in which they recorded everything from the latest gossip about the preacher's wife to the beauty of the frost on the pumpkin patch. Plus they wrote letters, thousands and thousands of letters, to folks back home. The Texas postal service was not swift; it was not even reliable. But writing letters made these quietly brave women feel connected to the world they might never again rejoin.

In the following letter written in 1846, a young woman named Caroline pleads with her boyfriend to put an end to her misery and to return home.

Frontier men spent a lot of time in the saddle and away from home, leaving womenfolk to fend for themselves (William Samuel, *Man on Horseback*, oil, ca. 1860. Courtesy of the Alamo).

My dear Ichabod,

How I want to see your big grey eyes. O, how horror stricken am I at your long absence. I want to see you and feel your heart bump. Oh, sweet Ichabod, now do come out and let us get married if you love me. God bless you, if you are not sufficiently blest in being so sweet. Oh you marry-gold, you hollyhock, you tulip, you cabbage. Oh you sweet owl, do come and comfort your dying, sorrow smitten Caroline. Oh Ichabod, but how I do love your big red lips. Oh, you trim, tall fellow, full of manna of sweet love, how I do want to see you, you moddle of perfection. You have been gone this two months, and to me, poor me, it does seem like a hundred years. Your dear presence would to me be more than the cooling spring to the parched traveller of the desert; more than the green grass to the hungry ox; more than the pebbled pool to the wanton duck; yes more than a lump of sugar to a spoiled child! Why then will you not come, yes, fly as swift as the lightening to kiss the tear from the dimpled cheeks of your mad love. Oh bleak and wild is the house, the garden, the woods, and the world without thee. Oh, yes, bless thee, my dumplin, my jew-sharp, my all, my rooster my gentleman.

Caroline

Originally printed in the Clarksville Northern Standard, *July 8, 1846. Reprinted in* The Texas Republic: A Social and Economic History, *William Ransom Hogan, University of Oklahoma Press, 1946.*

Unit Six

AFTER HOURS

Not all Texas settlers wore buckskin and moccasins. In this painting, the artist depicts himself as guiding the ox wagon that holds the rest of his well-dressed family (Friedrich Richard Petri, *Going Visiting*, watercolor, 1853, Texas Memorial Museum. Courtesy Russell Fish, III).

Chapter 20
GOING VISITING

In the log cabin days of Texas, how did the women amuse themselves? There were no movie theaters, no malls, no skating rinks or gyms, no public entertainments at all except the occasional fancy dress ball held during the sitting of the legislature. Anyway, who had time to play? From dawn to dusk, frontier women had corn to grind, thread to weave, cows to milk, chickens to feed, clothes to mend, and children to watch.

Every once in a while, when it got to be too much, the women gathered up their children, grabbed the sampler they were embroidering, packed a cold chicken lunch, and hitched the mule to the carriage. Let their husbands spend the day in whatever manner they wished, cutting bee trees or killing bears, perhaps. They were going visiting.

W. C. Walsh was about seven years old when his mother took him visiting on a hot day in Austin in 1842. It was a day he never forgot.

In those days, when there were but few women in the settlement, it was the custom for all hands to visit and "spend the day" with each other. Each mother took her family of cubs with her and the event was as much enjoyed by the children as by the grown folks.

One warm summer day the hosts gathered at the home of Mrs. Ann Wooldridge on the west side of the Avenue, below Sixth Street. She had a roomy house and, best of all, a large backyard in which to pen the boys. After dinner, the boys gathered in this enclosure and some one of them suggested that we slip off and go swimming. No one who has ever been a boy will be surprised to learn that we yielded to the temptation. The point selected was Shoal Creek, at the point now crossed by the International Railroad. We were but a short time in reaching the point and a much shorter time in stripping off our clothes and plunging in.

On the west bank of the creek, in what was later known as the "Raymond Plateau," and now covered by the compress, was a small field of corn. A man by the name of Fox was at work in the field and was regarded by us as a guarantee from danger. There was never a bunch of happier, disobedient kids assembled.

Suddenly, above our screams and laughter, there came to us a cry of mortal terror. One of our number ran up the east bank and saw half a dozen Indians surrounding Fox, shooting arrows and thrusting spears into his body. To yell, "Injuns! Injuns!" and start for town was the work of only seconds and to follow him, screaming and naked, through tall grass and weeds was a still shorter job for the whole crowd.

Just as we started on our nude race we heard the "Indian alarm" drum beating and our mothers heard it, too. As one woman they rushed to the west door to find the yard empty. The following few minutes witnessed a scene that is simply past description. Each mother knew, without a doubt, that her boy was either dead—or worse—a prisoner in the hands of the Indians.

Fortunately our speed and screams soon disclosed the fact that at least some of us had escaped. As, one by one, we appeared in sight, the mother of each grabbed her darling in her arms and covered him with kisses.

I don't know, but I am inclined to think that our naked bodies were temptations too strong to be resisted, for, in a short time, each mother, with tear-stained cheeks, was spanking her darling boy.

Never having been a mother, this proceeding is still a mystery to me.

"Austin in the Making," W. C. Walsh, The Austin Statesman, February 3, 1924. Courtesy Austin American Statesman.

Chapter 21
THE FIDDLER

Frontier Texans were passionate about dancing. Doing the "double shuffle" and "cutting the pigeon's wing" was great therapy for ragged nerves. Stationing a guard at the door of the party kept Indians at bay. Loud violin music blocked out any random sounds of gunfire that might keep the guests from having a good time. For a few blissful hours, the dancers were safe within the four walls of their wooden cocoon.

What would a dance be without music? These East Texas folks found out for themselves.

But now a dilemma occurred which entirely spoiled the sport of those who up to this time had had "no show" whatever—the fiddler, who had been imbibing rather copiously of whiskey, was found to be so drunk that he could not sit upon a chair, much less draw a tune from his violin. The lower classes were in sore distress, as no other musician could be found. They rolled the drunken man upon the floor, they stirred him up, they rubbed his head with vinegar, and they crammed an entire jar of Underwood's pickles down his throat—but all would not do.

At this juncture, and when the poorer people had given up all in despair, their spirits were suddenly elated by an offer on the part of Capt. H., provided they could procure him the fiddle, to give them a tune. . . .

Although by 1846 nearly every Texas settlement boasted at least one piano, the most common musical instrument was the fiddle (William Henry Huddle, *Old Slave*, oil, ca. 1889, Dallas Museum of Art, The Karl and Esther Hoblitzelle Collection, gift of the Hoblitzelle Foundation).

The dancers were in ecstacies, the fiddle was procured, and a cotillion set was immediately formed on the floor. Capt. H. was in no particular hurry, but continued his flourishes in the way of tuning the instrument for some time. Once or twice he drew the bow scientifically across the strings, which were now horribly out of tune—flourishes which caused the eager dancers immediately to commence "forwarding" across the floor but the waggish captain had no intention of giving them a "send off" so suddenly.

At length, thinking he had infused a sufficiency of the effervescence of dancing into the eager set, he drew the cork by giving every string on the violin a general rake with the bow. Away they went like mad, Capt. H. still sawing away, stamping his right foot as if keeping time, and calling the figure. Never was there seen such a dance. "Chassez," "cross over," "dos-a-dos," were called out by the captain, amid a series of sounds from the punished violin which would set a professor crazy; but so full of dance were the head and foot couple that they carried the thing through with as much zeal as though they had been bitten by Italian tarantulas.

It may readily be supposed that the dancers had but a limited knowledge of music; but still they could tell, in their cooler moments, a tune from a tornado. The first two couples had by this time finished, and the second had commenced, when one of the former addressed his partner with:

"Eliza, did you ever hear that tune he's a-playin afore?"

"Can't say that I ever has," was the response, and this within hearing of Capt. H, who was still punishing the violin as severely as ever.

"Does it sound to you like much of a tune, Eliza, anyhow?"

"Well, it doesn't."

"Nor to me either," said the first speaker, who all the while had his head turned to one side after the manner of a hog listening. "My opinion is that that feller there is naterally jest promiscuously and miscellaneously sawin away without exactly knowin what he's a doin."

This was too much for the captain, who now dropped the violin and rushed from the room and sought his quarters for the night. Thus ended a ball in Eastern Texas.

"Life in Eastern Texas—Dancing to a Strange Tune," New Orleans Daily Picayune, *March 11, 1843.*

Chapter 22
THE FANDANGO

In 1844, a group of French-Alsatian immigrants traveled to San Antonio where, for a few months, they awaited the arrival of their leader, Henri Castro. Once united, they planned to travel west to the banks of the cypress-shaded Medina River and establish a new colony. They would call it "Castro-ville."

San Antonio was nothing like their native France. The market plaza was crammed with mule trains, vendors, and oxcart drivers shouting in Spanish, "¡Andele! ¡Andele!" as they prodded their cattle with long sticks. Mexican women knelt in dusty doorways kneading tortillas on stone metates. On Sunday mornings, men met in the shadow of San Fernando Cathedral to bet on bloody cockfights.

At least two French-Alsatian immigrants were fascinated by these new and exotic scenes. One night, Auguste Frétellière and the artist, Théodore Gentilz, decided to attend a Mexican fandango. Here is Auguste's recollection of that fandango, along with a copy of Théodore's painting.

We had often heard of the fandango. We resolved, Théodore and I, to go to one, and toward ten o'clock of a certain evening we walked over to Military Plaza. The sound of the violin drew us to the spot where the fête was in full swing. It was in a rather large room of an adobe house, earthen floored, lighted by six-tallow candles placed at equal distances from each other. At the back, a

Dancing was by far the most popular form of entertainment in early Texas. The roughness of cabin floors made gliding impossible, giving way to new and livelier dance styles (Jean Louis Théodore Gentilz, *Fandango*, oil, 1848, Daughters of the Republic of Texas Library at the Alamo, San Antonio).

great chimney in which a fire of dry wood served to reheat the *café,* the tamales, and enchiladas: opposite, some planks resting on frames, and covered with a cloth, formed a table on which cups and saucers were set out.

A Mexican woman in the forties, with black hair, dark even for her race, bright eyes, and extraordinary activity, above all with the most agile of tongues—such was Doña Andrea Candelaria, patroness of the fandango. At the upper end of the room, seated on a chair which had been placed on an empty box, was the music, which was a violin. That violinist had not issued from a conservatory, but on the whole he played in fairly good time. He was called Paulo, and being blind, played from memory. The airs, for the most part Mexican, were new to me.

The women were seated on benches placed on each side of the room. The costumes were very simple, dresses of light colored printed calico, with some ribbons. All were brunettes with complexions more or less fair, but generally they had magnificent black eyes which fascinated me.

As for the men, they wore usually short jackets, wide-brimmed hats, and nearly all the Mexicans wore silk scarfs, red or blue or green, around their waists.

The dance which I liked best was called the quadrille. It is a waltz in four-time with a step crossed on very slow measure. The Mexicans are admirably graceful and supple.

When the quadrille is finished, the cavalier accompanies his partner to the buffet, where they are served a cup of coffee and cakes. Then he conducts the young lady to her mother or to her chaperone to whom the girl delivers the cakes that she has taken care to reap at the buffet. The mother puts them in her handkerchief, and if the girl is pretty and has not missed a quadrille, the mama carries away an assortment of cakes to last the family more than a week.

Finally we went home, very content with our evening, and promising ourselves to return another time.

Reprinted with permission from Castro-Ville and Henry Castro, Empresario, *Julia Nott Waugh,* p. 93, c. 1934. *Courtesy of the Castro Colonies Heritage Association.*

A savage brawl was often the Texan way of handling a duel (Artist unknown, *Sporting Anecdotes. Fighting it Out* or *The Colonel and the Kentucky Boatman. 'Hello, Friend, don't Forget that Vote,'* engraving, ca. 1839. San Jacinto Museum of History, La Porte, Texas).

Chapter 23
BRIT BAILEY

Brit Bailey loved to fight. Although lame and hoarse, he was considered "one tough hombre." Often, out of sheer boredom, he would wander around Brazoria until he found what he was itching for—a fight. He jumped right in, shouting, "Free fight, boys!" never bothering to ask what the fight was even about.

Brit Bailey was one of the "ring-tailed roarers" who moved to Texas in the early nineteenth century. They valued brawn, not brains, and loved proving themselves in combat. They boasted that they were "half-horse and half-alligator" and could live on "rotgut whiskey and bear's meat" that was "salted in a hailstorm, peppered with buckshot, and broiled in a flash of forked lightning." They fought with pistols and giant Bowie knives they kept strapped to their sides or stuck in their boot tops. Often, though, they simply fought with what came naturally—their fists.

Here is the legend of that famous "ring-tailed roarer" from Texas, Brit Bailey, written in 1934.

Tradition has it that Briton Bailey preceded Stephen F. Austin to the enchanted domain later known as Austin's Colony; in fact it has been stated by many of the old timers of Brazoria County, that Bailey was an officer in the service of Lafitte; and when the latter gentleman, at the earnest solicitation of Lieutenant Kearney of the United States Navy, removed himself and followers from

Galveston Island, Briton Bailey, like many others of the crew, located along the coast of Texas.

Now it was reported that Bailey built for himself a substantial residence, at a place the present location of which is known as Bailey's Prairie in Brazoria County; this place being on the left side of the road leading from Angleton to Brazoria just after emerging from the Oyster Creek woods.

Briton Bailey had the reputation of being a fearless man; and by a few as a just one. He was a very hard drinker and all-in-all, what might be termed from present day standards a desperate character. He had a very beautiful daughter of whom he was extremely fond and very jealous; and upon returning to his home one evening he was surprised at finding Stephen F. Austin in company with his daughter.

In no uncertain terms and emphatic language, he suggested to Austin his presence in that locality was not desired and could be easily dispensed with. Probably this is the cause that prompted the letter . . . from Austin to Bailey a few days after this incident [asking Bailey to leave his colony—October 3, 1823, letter from Stephen F. Austin to James B. Bailey]. Or it may have been that the letter was prompted by the tradition that, after a few hours after the time Austin reluctantly bade farewell to the fair daughter of Mr. Bailey at the latter's request, the two men met face-to-face in the road leading towards San Felipe de Austin, at which time and place Bailey held his cocked rifle on Austin and coaxed the Empresario to knock the back step and cut the pigeon wing for a period of about two hours.

It seems to be a fact that Briton Bailey did not comply with Austin's request and remove himself and family from the colony as is evidenced by the fact that on July 7, 1824, almost a year subsequent to the date of the letter from Austin to Bailey, a title to one league of land was issued to James B. Bailey as a citizen of Austin's colony. . . .

There is a story which the old time darkies of Oyster Creek declare to be true to the effect that Briton Bailey and a man by the name of Smith for many years lived in that vicinity together in the house which Bailey had built; but after many years of close friendship a very heated quarrel arose between the two, and at the request of Bailey, Smith left the country vowing at the time that he would return some day and put an end to Bailey; and that in the event Bailey should die before Smith's return, he would dig up the body and fill it full of lead.

Believing that Smith would carry out his promise exactly as he had agreed if he should ever return, and desiring to forestall such an incident, Bailey gave orders just before his death to his wife and children that his body be buried standing up facing west, his cocked rifle in his hands, and a jug of whiskey at his feet. His orders were obeyed and his request was granted; his body was buried at his family home on Bailey's Prairie in Brazoria County, Texas.

Judge Walter M. Caldwell of Houston says that many of the old time residents of Bailey's Prairie and all of the older darkies will verify the truthfulness of his statements that on dark or rainy nights, and near the spot where Briton Bailey was buried standing on his feet, there can frequently be seen a white figure moving to and fro carrying a lantern around, apparently looking for some lost object. Whether this ghost or other nocturnal figure was the spirit of Stephen F. Austin returned to the haunts of his earthly days in search of his long lost love; whether it was the man, Smith, returned to carry out his promise; or whether it was Briton Bailey guarding the welfare of his family and his property in that same efficient manner as he did while on earth, no one knows.

But Judge Caldwell declares that many years ago as a bare foot boy, when he tramped about Bailey's Prairie after dark, he, on all occasions, traveled at maximum speed; and even at the present time, when he passes through Bailey's Prairie after dark, he never feels quite at ease unless his car is running at full speed.

The present day citizens of Oyster Creek and Bailey's Prairie will tell you that on dark and rainy nights, they have often observed a light on the prairie which they have never been able to understand or explain. It is next to impossible to get one of the old time negroes of that vicinity to venture out on Bailey's Prairie after dark.

Bailey (James B.) vertical file, The Center for American History, The University of Texas at Austin.

Der Unvermeidliche

Gentlemen relax in the friendly atmosphere of a German saloon in New Braunfels (Carl von Iwonski, *Der Unvermeidliche (The Unavoidable)*, engraving, 1855, Institute of Texan Cultures, San Antonio. Courtesy of Mrs. W. D. McKee).

Chapter 24
STAGECOACH INN

Leopold von Iwonski did not leave Germany in 1845 intending to run a stagecoach inn in Texas. He had been quite content just cultivating his fields of corn, peas, and sweet potatoes on his farm at the Guadalupe River ford just outside New Braunfels. The Iwonski farm was prosperous, as anyone passing by could see. Many people were passing by: the Iwonski farm was situated on a stagecoach route. In no time, travelers who had left Austin on the early morning stage began appearing on Iwonski's doorstep hungry, thirsty, and exhausted.

Iwonski embraced them with open arms. By 1850, the Iwonski House had become a regular stage stop on the San Antonio-Austin route and a popular recreation center. It was the scene of many amusing incidents, one of which is recorded here by another German emigrant who settled in Sisterdale, Julius Dresel.

On the next evening, we busied ourselves in dedicating the tap room of Captain von Iwonski in a fitting manner. Aside from a table and benches, there were pyramids of colored, empty and water-filled bottles ranged round the room. The host had been warned and had borrowed whiskey, sugar, and lemons from Ferguson's store, and as we were considerate enough to ask only for whiskey straight, whiskey punch, whiskey toddy, or for a change, lemonade, the entertainment ran off smoothly until there suddenly appeared in our midst three elegantly dressed emigrants from South Carolina bound for the land of gold, California, by way of Texas, the desert, and across the Gila and Colorado Rivers. They were encamped in the town of Comal.

One of the three, under the influence of liquor, surprised me by asking, "Did you ever kill a man?" whereat I answered that it was not customary to kill one's fellow men in Germany. Whereupon, he went up to the wall lamp to light his cigar, but as this could not be done because of the shade, he, angrily, threw down the lamp with the words, "Your damned German fire does not burn!" pulled out a beautifully decorated dagger, gesticulated with it, and yelled, "I want to kill somebody!" which did not sound very consoling, especially when you are wearing a very white vest over your shirt.

We asked the other two to please remove their benevolent companion, but they were hardly on the street when we heard swearing and scolding in German and there followed—"slap, slap"—two loud boxes on the ear for the man with the dagger who wanted to cool his anger on the favorite cow of a woman neighbor. As for the rest, the culprit came the next day to apologize and to pay for the damages.

Julius Dresel Notebook, 1850. Texana/Geneology, San Antonio Public Library.

Unit Seven

ANIMALIA

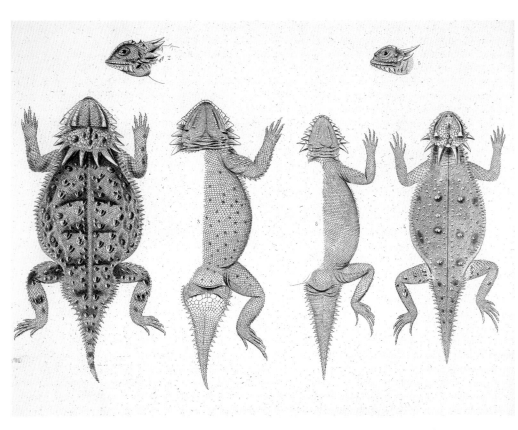

Horned lizards (more frequently, but inaccurately, called horny toads) were once the pocket pet of choice among Texas schoolchildren. They knew that these animals liked to have their tummies tickled and had "no more malice than there is in a cauliflower" (J. H. Richard, *Phrynosoma Regale and Doliosaurus Mc'Calli*, engraving, 1858, *United States and Mexican Boundary Survey Under the Order of Lieutenant Colonel W. H. Emory, Major First Cavalry, and United States Commissioner*. CT0086, Center for American History, University of Texas at Austin).

Chapter 25
THE EXTRAORDINARY TEXAS
HORNY TOAD

On December 29, 1839, a young and elegant Irishman set sail with his terrier, Nelly, from Barbados. He was bound for the Republic of Texas. He was Francis C. Sheridan, a British diplomat. His job was to observe firsthand the "character and habits of the Texans" and report back to the British government which was, at that time, considering whether or not to officially recognize the new republic.

At first it did not seem that Sheridan could adjust to life in Galveston. He had not expected the weather there to be so cold. A blue norther had welcomed Her Majesty's ship, "Pilot," into the Gulf of Mexico and Francis had packed only light, tropical clothing. He had been forced to borrow pants from the Corporal of Marines, a jacket from the Captain, and gloves from the Master. To this rough getup, he added a yellow neckerchief. He made his first appearance before the citizens of the Republic dressed like a common sailor.

Within no time, however, Sheridan was drawn into the Texan way of life. He was, perhaps, a little charmed by it, too. In his diary, he dutifully recorded the local habits, one of which, we discover, he adopted as his very own.

Texas abounds with game such as Buffalo, Deer, &c and I have heard that the cheetar is to be found. Wild Turkey, Praiarie Hen, Goose, Duck, Snipe, &c are in abundance. . . . The Rattle Snake is common enough, but is thought little of by the inhabitants in comparison with "the Copper headed snake," the bite of w^h [which] instantly attended to, is certain death. . . .

But the most extraordinary creature I ever saw is what is here in great abundance termed "the Horned Frog"*—Of w^h I have two specimens now. It is tail & all about 6 inches long having the head of a frog, the back & belly of an alligator, & the tail of a turtle—at least these are the best comparisons w^h at this moment strike me. They also possess the abstinence of the chamelion, & will remain a very long time without food of any sort for 90 days. However as I want to preserve mine if possible to a good old age I treat them to a light diet of flies of w^h I find they are fond.

Their rations in the cold season when flies are scarce, are 3 blue-bottles per diem & at one time I was necessitated to reduce this to one (on w^h the judgment of Solomon was executed) equally divided between both. At this time however they are very well off, & very frequently I am enabled to afford the luxury of a musquito w^h serves as a variety to their frugal meal, and when by a generous but judiciously regulated diet, I have strengthened the tone of their Stomachs, I intend to allow cock-roaches twice a week & every other Sunday. And of these God Knows they need not doubt but that they have the best & freshest in the Market.

Their House is Spacious, & the accommodations as they say of Hotels "in every way worthy of the building w^h is a cigar box capable of containing 250 "weeds." At the bottom of this I have strewn a bed of rushes, varied with little lumps of mud & on these I have ingeniously contrived to throw a mellow light, by the assistance of a covering of whity brown paper through w^h In imitation of Gothic architecture I have pierced "arrow slits." So that by the slightest "nudge" from the elbow of imagination they may fancy themselves in the vicinity of some lost and lamented puddle. The heart of Frog can desire no more.

From Galveston Island Or, A Few Months Off the Coast of Texas: The Journal of Francis C. Sheridan, 1839-1840, *ed. by Willis W. Pratt, 1954, pp. 102-104. By permission of the University of Texas Press.

The Texas horned lizard (or horny toad) is now a protected species. Few remain in the wild. Its main food source, western harvester ants, has been decimated by the insecticides used to kill fire ants.

Chapter 26
HOG-KILLING TIME

Hogs were the settlers' insurance against famine. They were so easy to raise on the frontier. For most of the year, they were let loose in the woods to scavenge for their own food. Texas was a banquet of grubs, worms, insects, snakes, roots, nuts, fruit, and mice, so the pigs ate well. When the weather turned cooler and the winter neared, they were rounded up at the farm and "shucked-up" with generous helpings of corn.

"Hog-killin' time" was a happy celebration. In the following account, Amzina Wade recalls what it was like growing up as a white child on a prosperous Texas plantation before the Civil War.

Coming in quick succession after cotton marketing came "hog-killing time," a prelude of the Christmastide and much of the same exhilarating, happy air flowing up and down and around the plantation life. The fattening pens were at the big spring for convenience in slaughtering. We children, my sister and I and numerous cousins were always in evidence on these vastly interesting occasions, always hanging around, patiently tolerated I think, as an inevitable nuisance but sharers in the zestful good feeling that prevailed.

The negro boys were busy roasting kidneys and bits of tenderloin in the hot ashes around the scalding kettles, collecting the bladders, blowing them big and full like a toy balloon, tying

The first frost of November or December signaled the beginning of hog-killing time (H. O. Kelly, *Hog-Killing Time*, oil, ca. 1950, Dallas Museum of Art, Dallas Art Association Purchase).

securely and carefully hanging away to dry and later to serve as Christmas guns.

The hogs were slaughtered, scraped, and cleaned, then dexterously carved. We were intensely interested in each operation, but the great tubs of sausage claimed our chief attention for therein lay the choicest, the tastiest, and most relished of the various kinds of meat. You have all seen these present day sausage mills and eaten and relished the peppery and herb-seasoned meat but in the perfection of its preparation you have lacked a long way of tasting and seeing the sausage made in my childhood, when mills for grinding the meat were unknown.

Then, there were sawed from the trunks of the largest trees, blocks of convenient height and in the smooth surface of the upper end was dug and hollowed out a deep, rounding hole, a mortar, and into this the meat cut into small bits was thrown from the tubs. A strong negro man on either side, with a heavy wooden pestle would beat and pound it into a smooth pulp, not a lump or solid piece in the whole mass, the seasoning was then carefully and thoroughly worked in, you had indeed a dish fit for the most fastidious epicurian taste, stimulating, satisfying, delightful, nothing lacking.

You children know what a Southern Christmas means, the Yule fires brightly burning, good cheer, good will, good humor pervading every nook and corner, blowing and billowing over all the world. It is Christmas indeed. Christmas glee and glow, Christmas spirit filled to overflowing, every heart.

"*Recollections of a Child's Life on a Pioneer Plantation,*" *Amzina Wade,* Chronicles of Smith County, Texas, *vol. xix, no. 2 (Winter, 1980). Courtesy of Smith County Historical Society.*

Children found no shortage of things to do—or not to do—in the country-side of early Fredericksburg (Hermann Lungkwitz, *View of Friedrichsburg, Texas,* 1859, engraving, accession number 1974.14, Amon Carter Museum, Fort Worth, Texas).

Chapter 27
TWO BOYS AND A PANTHER

When Frederick Law Olmsted traveled through Texas in 1854, it was a hunter's paradise. In abundance, turkey, deer, red cattle, buffalo, and wild hogs roamed the countryside. Scouting for supper too far from home, though, spelled danger for the hunters. But the settlers of Texas were a different breed; they were not easily frightened. On the contrary, it was the danger which heightened the thrill of the hunt.

In this next passage, Olmsted remembers meeting two such hardy pioneers, both of them teenagers, who lived in a German settlement just south of Fredericksburg.

Evening found us in the largest house of the settlement, and a furious norther suddenly rising, combined with the attractive reception we met . . . compel(led) us to stay two days without moving.

Mr. D., our host, was a man of unusually large education, and, having passed some years at school in England, spoke English in perfection. Before the Revolution he had controlled an estate on which the taxes were $10,000. He had become a popular leader, and was placed at the head of the temporary government of his Duchy. When the reaction came, all was swept away, and, exiling himself, he came to settle here. Now, working with his own hands in the Texan backwoods, he finds life not less pleasant than before.

His house stands upon a prominence, which commands the beautiful valley in both directions. His fields are just below. He had this year cultivated sixty acres, and with the help of the forenoons of his two sons, of fourteen and fifteen, who are at school the rest of the day, had produced 2,500 bushels of corn, besides some cotton, wheat, and tobacco.

These sons were as fine pictures of youthful yeomen as can be imagined—tall, erect, well knit, with intelligent countenances, spirited, ingenuous, gentle, and manly. In speaking of his present circumstances, he simply regretted that he could not give them all the advantages of education that he himself had. But he added that he would much rather educate them to be independent and self-reliant, able and willing to live by their own labor, than to have them ever feel themselves dependent on the favor of others. . . .

Our supper was furnished by the boys, in the shape of a fat turkey from the river bottoms. This one made eighty-five that had been shot by them during the winter. Among other feats of theirs at the gun, we were told of two adventures with panthers.

Made aware, at dusk, one night, by the dogs, that something unusual was around the house, the two boys started with their guns to see what it might be. Light enough was left to show them a panther, who retreated, and, pressed by the dogs, took to a tree in the bottoms. He was ensconced in the branches of a cotton-wood that hung obliquely over the stream. It was too dark to see his exact position, and taking places upon the bent trunk, to prevent his descent, the boys agreed to keep guard till the moon rose. But they were tired with work, and daylight found them both asleep where they were—the panther missing! He had either walked over their bodies or dropped into the river.

On the other occasion, the boys were alone with their mother, Mr. D. having gone on a two or three days excursion. They were awakened in the night by a stir about the out-houses. There had been signs of a panther about the hog-yard for several days, and they sprang out as they were, seizing their guns, in the hope of putting an end to the marauds.

The night was pitchy dark, and stealing cautiously along, they came suddenly upon an enormous panther, within a few yards of the door. The panther gave one bound into a tree, probably more startled than themselves. He was quite invisible, and perfectly still. One of the boys thought of a lantern, and, running back, found his mother already up and alarmed.

"A lantern," he shouted, in a furious whisper, and ran back to the tree.

The mother appeared with the lantern at the door, and came, in her night-dress, to the tree. What would she have thought at court, five years before, of holding a lantern, to shoot a panther? She held it high. Both boys took slow aim at the glaring eye-balls, which alone were visible above them. One pulled; the gun snapped. A quick jerk of the eye-balls gave warning of a spring, when a ball from the other rifle brought the panther dead to their feet.

It proved, by daylight, the largest that had been known in the settlement, measuring nine feet from nose to tip of tail, and weighing, by estimate, 250 lbs.

From A Journey Through Texas Or, A Saddle-Trip on the Southwestern Frontier, *Frederick Law Olmsted*, pp. 196-198, 1989. *By permission of the University of Texas Press.*

The Spanish mustang or wild horse was prized for its endurance (William Tylee Ranney, *Hunting Wild Horses*, oil, 1846, Autry Museum of Western Heritage, Los Angeles).

Chapter 28
MUSTANG CATCHING

Immense herds of wild horses called mustangs, descendants of horses brought to America by the Spanish conquistadores, once populated the Texas plains. John C. Duval, a survivor of the Goliad Massacre, recalls encountering one such herd in the 1840s.

[I saw] . . . a drove of mustangs so large that it took us fully an hour to pass it, although they were traveling at a rapid rate in a direction nearly opposite to ours. As far as the eye could extend on a dead level prairie, nothing was visible except a dense mass of horses, and the trampling of their hoofs sounded like the roar of the surf on a rocky coast.

From The Young Explorers, John C. Duval, Austin, 1892.

Mustang catching was big business for frontiersmen. It wasn't easy, but if you had a lot of time on your hands, patience, a decent saddle, and just a dash of horse sense, the mustangs brought

good money, as Wilson Jones of Floydada informs us in the following story.

Reprint courtesy of the Fort Worth Star-Telegram.

I decided to get on out West when I was 17, rode the train to Colorado City, caught a ride on a wagon a piece farther on, then a man leading a horse let me ride the lead horse until we got to a ranch. I got a job here, on the Yellowhouse, tending sheep, till I could get enough money to buy me a saddle. I was willing to walk until I could ride. Caught the measles there, but wasn't very sick. Remember the rancher brought me a jug of whisky from Beach Grocery Store for medicine.

Got enough money together to buy a saddle, got jobs here and there. In the Fall of 1887 I worked for Perry Merrill in Floyd County, on the Blanco Canyon. He wanted someone to keep mustangs away from his horses.

The mustangs would run off the gentle work horses. Merrill and I built a corral and caught four or five mustangs. He would sell them to cowboys going home in the fall. He paid me by cutting out four or five broncs and letting me take my pick, one a month. I broke 'em and would get from $30 to $40 a head, easy.

Well, about the mustang catching. Wes Poke and his brother Warren were batchin' up the canyon and wanted me to catch mustangs for them. I rode around and hunted up the biggest batch of mustangs that ran solid, that is, stuck together in one herd. Was two weeks locating one that suited me. The morning sun was coming up when I started after them. Don't know how far I rode that day, from a trot to a lope, half speed all day. The herd started north, swung back toward where Lubbock is now, and night caught me close to old Della Plains with only 16 head. All day they had kept splitting off and losing out. I got back to 10 or

15 miles from where I started. Next morning by 10 o'clock I had them together again. I went to camp to eat a little something and change horses. After that I would eat and change horses when I could.

And do you know what, every time I went out on a fresh horse, them mustangs would run again. After three or four days of this sort of worryin' around, the bunch broke for the Tierra Blanca, near Hereford, with me right after them. There were 11 little colts in the bunch. The mothers kept dragging back with them. Another bunch of wild horses came out of a lake and began fighting with my bunch and I had to let a number of them swing off, but the next day I picked them up again.

I kept this up, a' follerin' and a' follerin' and eating when I could. For about 15 days I kept them on a run, letting them drink all the water they could hold in the daytime so they could graze and rest at night. Kept crowdin' them so they couldn't graze in the daytime. Long 'bout the fifteenth day I left them in a lake and went to camp. Wes had been to Estacado, the Quaker town, and bought some rope and a sight of rivets and leather from old man Hammack, the bootmaker.

The next day when I started to bring the horses in they turned and ran. I was riding old Selam, one of Wes' best horses, and I turned and rode around them and whooped and hollered to make them turn. I never carried a gun to shoot off to make them turn, just worked and fooled with them. Well, that night I had them in about a mile of the wagon. For three or four days we kept them on the go, a mile or so, then back, then we put them on the milling ground, and soon that acre or so was nothing but a dust bed. We put ropes on the ground until they got used to them. At first when their feet would touch a rope they would jump as far as they could.

The next thing was to get them used to a man. We put a cedar post about a hundred yards away and Wes took his seat on the ground by it. A long rope stretched from the post to the milling ground, with a small loop in the end. I rode round and round the milling 'ground. Hundreds of times they would spy the loop, but every now and then we got a horse. When the horse was standing with his tail toward Wes and his foot in the loop, Wes jerked the rope and the loop came up nice round his front leg.

The first horse we caught reared and lunged. I swung a rope on him and the cook saw the herd getting away, so he came and held them. We threw the wild horse down and branded him, then put a clog on his foot. A clog is a chain fastened to the horse's front legs by a piece of leather, riveted on. Now here is where we made our first mistake. Walter Harris, an old mustang catcher in Colorado, had told me how it was done, but he didn't tell me one thing. He didn't tell me not to turn our first clogged horse loose. We did, and he ran into the bunch, fell and stampeded them, and it took between sundown and dark to get them together again.

Walter Harris said he owned most of the little towns in Western Kansas—traded mustangs for them. He afterward told me he never had caught a bunch as big as that one and that he never would give away his secret of catching mustangs again. He was a great joker.

Well, anyway, we caught the horses that same way, three to four a day mostly, biggest lot in one day was seven. We got every one in that bunch, 56 in all, and never crippled or killed a one. We were just lucky.

"Pioneer Tells Graphic Story of Wild Horse Catching Fifty Years Ago in Texas," Fort Worth Star-Telegram, February 27, 1941.

Unit Eight

GROWING PAINS

Cynthia Ann Parker is shown here nursing her daughter and wearing her hair short—a Comanche sign of mourning (Photographer unknown, *Cynthia Ann Parker, Fort Worth, Texas, 1861*, Western History Collections, University of Oklahoma, Norman).

Chapter 29
CYNTHIA ANN PARKER

On May 18, 1836, Comanche and Kiowa warriors raided Fort Parker and kidnapped five people. One of the five captives was nine-year-old Cynthia Ann Parker. The Comanches took Cynthia Ann back to their camp where she was adopted by an Indian family. They renamed her "Naduah." Years went by and Cynthia Ann did not see another white face. She gradually forgot her native manners, customs, and language. She indeed became Naduah.

Naduah grew up to be an attractive woman, catching the eye of the respected war chief, Peta Nocona, and becoming his wife. She bore him two sons and a baby girl, Topasannah (Prairie Flower), later nicknamed "Tecks Ann."

Naduah lived twenty-four years with the roving Comanche band called the Wanderers, never spending more than three or four days in one place. Like the other squaws, she was expected to erect tepees, herd horses, tend children, load pack-mules, dress animal skins, cook buffalo meat, and gather wild fruit and berries for food and dyes. And, when night came, she slept on the ground covered only by a buffalo skin. It became the only life she knew.

But that all changed one cold, foggy morning in December 1860 when Texas rangers under Captain (and later, Governor) Sul Ross swooped down on her Comanche band camped in the Pease River Valley. Caught unawares, many of the Indians were killed as they fled. Naduah, with her infant daughter in her arms, mounted a fleet, iron-gray horse and raced to escape.

Almost the entire band was massacred. But not Naduah and her baby. Her horse was swift, but that was not what saved her. Although her face was browned by the sun and her blonde hair had been blackened with grease, the rangers could tell that she *was no blood Comanche. . . . "[T]his is a white woman, Indians do not have blue eyes," said Captain Ross. He spared her life and her baby's.*

Naduah and Topasannah were taken to Fort Cooper, where they were bathed, clothed, and comforted by the army wives. These wives had not forgotten the 1836 raid on Fort Parker; could this grown woman be the long-lost Cynthia Ann abducted as a child so many years before?

Cynthia Ann was reunited with her birth family, who were jubilant at her return. Cynthia Ann, nonetheless, was miserable, never adjusting to the settled life with the Parkers and grieving constantly for her two sons and husband she never saw again. She died in 1864. Some say she died of a broken heart, that she starved herself to death. One of Cynthia Ann's neighbors, T. J. Cates, recalls her last, melancholy days.

I well remember Cynthia Ann Parker and her little girl, Tecks Ann; she lived at the time about six miles south of Ben Wheeler, with her brother-in-law, Ruff O'Quinn, near Slater's Creek. She looked to be stout and weighed about 140 pounds, well-made, and liked to work. She had a wild expression and would look down when people looked at her. She could use an ax equal to a man and she liked to work, and disliked a lazy person. She was an expert in tanning hides with the hair on them, or plaiting or knitting either ropes or whips.

She thought her two boys were lost on the prairie after she was captured and would starve to death. This dissatisfied her very much, and she wanted to go back to the Indians. She would take a knife and hack her breast until it would bleed, then put the blood on some tobacco and burn it, and cry for her lost boys.

Almost every Sunday my wife would carry the Indian girl, Tecks Ann, visiting. She was pretty and smart, and was about three years of age the last time we saw her. She died and was buried in old Asbury graveyard about eight miles south of Ben Wheeler. Poor Cynthia Ann was grieved over the loss of her child and she then moved to Anderson County, where she soon died of la grippe. She was an open-hearted, good woman, and always ready to help somebody.

"Cynthia Ann Parker" T. J. Cates, Edgewood Journal, June 1918. Reprinted in Cynthia Ann Parker, Grace Jackson, The Naylor Co., 1959.

Postscript: One of Cynthia Ann's sons was Quanah Parker, the last of the great Comanche chiefs. Although he never saw his mother after her recapture, Quanah never forgot her and took her birth name, Parker, as his own. In 1910, he moved his mother's body from a Henderson County, Texas, cemetery to one in Oklahoma, so she could, at long last, be reunited with her Indian brethren.

Artist Charles Herff has captured the carnival atmosphere of a typical nineteenth-century public hanging (Charles Adelbert Herff, *The Hanging of Bob Augustin*, watercolor, ca. 1876, C. A. Herff Reminiscences, Prints and Photographs Collection, CT 0116, Center for American History, University of Texas at Austin).

Chapter 30
THE HANGING OF BOB AUGUSTIN

Texas vigilante groups often took justice into their own hands. Charles Herff was a small child when the following lynching took place in San Antonio in 1861. Here is his recollection.

Bob Augustin, a well known desperado, was one whom you would call an exceedingly good looking chap, about six feet tall slender and about thirty-five years old, as he had spent half his life on horseback, a slight bow-leggedness was noticeable, he always wore a large brown beautifully ornamented Mexican sombrero from under which his long wavy pitch black hair parted in the middle, fell gracefully over his broad shoulders, he had fine aristocratic features, nose slightly aquiline, brown expressive eyes with eye lashes at least half an inch long; a small black moustache and pearly white teeth set off his mouth which turned slightly upwards at the corners and often would he smile the smile of a bashful and innocent looking girl. . . .

[H]e always wore an immaculate clean white ruffled shirt and a red neck-tie about fifteen inches long, his coat was made from yellowish brown buckskin beautifully embroidered both front and back, a tribute of some of his many women admirers, both young & old, his pants were made of grey Corduroi, with fine black leather trimmings at the seam. Bobs boots were always highly polished, the top being adorned with a red Lone Star on a white background the bottom was finished with high heels to which were attached long clinking silver-trimmed Mexican spurs.

Bob as a rule was pleasant to engage in conversation but on the other hand in talking to someone who had incurred his displeasure that voice usually real musical and pleasing to the ear was suddenly transformed into a loud coarse, hard and grating one, at the same time his usual mellow eyes were transformed into a tiger like savage expression.

Anyway Bob Augustin was just the man a woman would fall in love with, he had a fine manly figure, he was strong and fearless, furthermore he was especially gallant and amiable to women yet with all these attributes and those soft gazelle like eyes back of them lured the unadulterated savage and demon, the least thing would rouse his ire and woe to him who got in his path the bullet for whom it was intended would always find its mark. . . .

Of course everybody was exceedingly courteous to Bob more out of fear than anything else, for every one knew that he was a very dangerous man to trifle with, nevertheless the Vigilantes kept their eyes on him. . . .

For some time Bob had behaved fairly well but all of a sudden it appeared he no longer could resist the temptation, he was bound to do something out of the ordinary, so one late Sunday afternoon he got on his fiery pinto mustang stallion and went over to the *Plaza de Armas* (Military Plaza) entered the *Cantina del Torro Verde* (The Green Bull Saloon) near San Pedro Creek on the Presidio (West Commerce Str.) took several drinks of Tequila, which started him a going some, from here he went over to Madam Candelarias Fandango, danced and swung some of the *Señoritas* around, drank some *Vino de Parral*, he became boisterous and hilarious, sang some ribald Spanish songs, then on horseback he went over to Chihuahua (Trans San Pedro district) attended a rooster and several dog fights and tanked up some more.

Now gloriously drunk he again swung on to his neighing mustang, he yelled and howled, shot out the lights in a certain Resort on East Street (now Santa Rosa Ave) shot off door knobs and at last deliberately shot a fleeing man in the leg and still mounted high on his neighing frothing stallion, he started away with lightning speed, turned abruptly off into Dolorosa Street and again rushing up to Military Plaza, he gave several blood-curdling wolf howls and still on horseback he charged the Chili stands (tables), knocked them over, he dismounted, chased the Chili queens (waitresses) in every direction, caught them by their long black tresses, whipped out his keen bladed Bowie knife and cut off their tresses which he then threw high into the air exultingly giving forth a most terrific horse laugh. . . .

[H]e was just having [a] riproaring glorious time but the ever vigilant Bill Lyons who was quite a distance away on Main Plaza, heard the commotion and at the risk of his life, rushed over, pounced upon Bob, caught him by his long hair, twisted his arms back of him and marched him off to the Bat Cave (Calaboose) [Courthouse and Jail].

It was about eight o'clock in the evening, but the news spread like wildfire; every body was told that the Vigilantes would get him in the morning and hang him of course I was not going to miss an event like this, nor were many other boys, who in spite of an anticipated flogging played hooky from school along with me.

THE TRIAL

Having the advantage of being a very slender boy I managed to squeeze myself through the dense crowd into the Court Room. The judge pro tem was sitting in the corner, with out-stre[t]ched legs, feet resting on the table, smoking his corncob pipe. . . . Just as I entered the room the acting Recorder said; "Mr. Seffel bring in Bob Augustin!" . . . Bob was brought in with his sombrero under his arm and took a seat directly opposite the judge.

The Judge: "Good morning Bob! Bob I see you done played hell again over there in Chihuahua last night. . . . You are charged with behavior unbecoming a gentleman. . . . [N]ow Bob I want to ask are you guilty or not guilty of these acts[?]"

Bob: "I refuse to answer and before you ask any more of them questions I want you to take them hoofs of yourn off the table out of consideration of the many refined ladies here present," the Judge reluctantly did so but there was a spontaneity of uproarious laughter, guffaw and applause[.]

The Judge got his dander up and with a vigorous whack struck his gavel on the table & bellowing out: "Order in Court." . . .

Judge: "Now Bob, I ask you again in all kindness are you guilty or not guilty of these charges[?]"

Bob: "You heard what I said before, its for you to find out, what the Hell are you here for any way" and with an oath and a terrific whack with his fist upon the table, he continued. "I want you to understand that I am a free born Texican and I demand a jury."

The Judge appeared some what surprised but said: "Seffel! go out there and bring in twelve men," after a delay of about an hour the twelve men came a shuffling in and the judge bade them to be seated. . . .

The Judge: "Gentlemen of this here jury! Bob Augustin is charged with playing Hell over in Chihuahua last night, firing off his six-shooters in every direction, shot a fleeing man in the . . ." and right here the judge was inter[r]upted by Bob.

"Judge hold that big trap of your'n a minute, I want to have a good look at this heah jury of mine. . . . Men! I tell you what I am up to, I am taking in my mind a photograph of you all, I want your faces so stamped on that brain of mine that I shall not forget and if you fellows dare to convict me, as sure as I, Bob Augustin is a sitting on this heah chair, I[']ll manage to git out of the Bat Cave and I[']ll make every one of you bite the dust" and then pointing his finger at the judge added: "Judge I want you to know this counts for you too, *Sabe!*" . . .

One of the jurors motioned to the judge to step nearer, they gathered in a cluster and after a brief delay the judge stepped forward and in a stentorian voice announced: "Bob! We have had a preliminary Pow-Wow in regard to your doings yesterday and we have decided that you are not guilty . . . you didn't kill nobody and whom we blame is that low down dog who sold you that rot gut (whiskey).". . .

Then the judge turned to Bob and said: "Bob you are discharged and you can go, you are now a free man." . . .

While the trial had been going on about two hundred men had assembled on the South side of the Plaza, Bob Augustin had not noticed them before. . . . Curiosity led him to put his head out the window to look at the crowd, immediately George Schroeder and Fritz Schreiner standing on the outside pounced upon him. . . .

The waiting crowd on the South side of the Plaza gave a tremendous shout and surged forward a yelling: "Hang him, Hang him! Break his bones in him! Skin him alive! Burn the ——." . . . Some one shouted: "Let's hang him yonder on one of them trees in front of the priest's house." . . .

Some of the men tore over to Moke's store and brought out two coils of rope, tied the ends to a tree then stretched it in a double row to two hitching posts and a Mexican carreta which happened to be standing there then back to another tree thereby forming a triangle within which Bob was placed under one of the trees, armed men got inside to keep the crowd off. . . .

Bobs hands were tied back of him but his legs were left free, the noose was put over his head, Richards tied the rope to the pummel of the saddle and was just about to pull him up. . . . Peñaloza tolled the bell at intervals of about three minutes to notify the waiting and nervous public.

For a while the crowd seemed puzzled but Peñaloza shouted: "Jacka! Yanka him ope!" Well! Bob went up and Peñaloza kept on ringing that bell more vigorously as Bob was going up and kept that bell a going for about half an hour after Bob breathed his last. . . .

All in all these happenings made such a terrible impression on my young mind that for about four months I would not sleep by myself but crept in with my oldest brother John. . . .

Of course as a great climax a good flogging awaited me for going to the hanging, next day to finish a good job about a dozen of my boy friends and I were flogged for playing hookey from school[.] Two days after the hangings Bishop Dupuys had twelve beautiful Elm trees cut down for fear there might be another hanging and as he said: it gave him ["]very much heart pain to pairceeve men hanging right in front of my door.["]

After the lynchings it was announced through hand bills and Posters as follows:

TAKE WARNING!

Henceforth Judges, Lawyers, Peace officers, Constables, Jurors and Citizens must not shirk their duty, if they fail to so a similar fate might befall them as did Bob Augustin and others.

Asa Mitchell   }   Representing three hundred or more law
José Peñaloza }   abiding citizens of San Antonio de Béxar

Herff (Charles Adelbert) Papers, The Center for American History, The University of Texas at Austin.

Chapter 31
MY SLAVE DAYS

Prior to the Civil War, 90 percent of Texas immigrants came from the Southern United States. Planters from Georgia and Mississippi came to Texas with dreams of empire—cotton empires. They brought with them their seeds and their slaves, who, by 1860, made up one-fourth of the Texas population. Under moss-hung oaks and beside muddy rivers, Texan planters built grand plantations and grew rich off the labor of their unpaid slaves.

Texas was no Land of Promise for the African-American slave. When she was only five years old, Francis Black was sold as a slave to a man from East Texas. Here she recalls her "slave days."

My name am Francis Black. I don't know jist how old I is, but I can 'member lots about slave days. I was a big girl, washing and ironing, when they sot [set] the darkies free. From that I "calculate" that I is in my eighties.

I was bo'n at Grand Bluff, Mississippi, on old man Tim Carltons' place. I was stold from my fo'ks when I was a little girl and never seed them no more. The kids played in the big road there in Mississippi. One day me and another girl was playing up and down the road and three white men come 'long in a wagon. They grabbed us up and put us in the wagon and civered [covered] us with quilts. I hollered and yelled and one of the men said, "Shut

In 1860, African-Americans made up one-fourth of the Texas population (Friedrich Richard Petri, *Hauling Water,* accession number 2270-3, water-color, ca. 1855. Courtesy of the Texas Memorial Museum, Austin).

up, you Nigger, or I'll kill you." I told him, "Kill me if you wants, you stole me from my fo'ks."

They took us to New Orleans to the slave market. I had long hair and they cut it off like a boys and tried to sell me. I told that man that was looking at us that the men cut my hair off, and that they stole me. The man who cut off my hair cursed me and said if I didn't hush he would kill me. The men who stole us couldn't sell us at New Orleans, and took us to Jefferson. I don't know what they done with the other girl. They sold me to Bill Tumlin. He run a big livery stable there at Jefferson. I belonged to the Tumlins till surrender.

I lived there in the house with them. They had a boy and girl and I was raised up round the house with them. They bought my clothes and took good care of me, but I never seed no money 'till after surrender. I et what they et after they got through. My Mistress allus saved me some of what they et. She say she didn't believe in feeding the darkies the scraps like some white fo'ks. The first work I done was washing and ironing.

Me and his two chil'ren played together. They was younger than me, and we used to fight mightily. When they fight me I fight them back, and scratch them up. Mistress Caroline use to say she was gwying [going] to thrash me if I didn't stop fighting her children. She never did — she was jist trying to scare me. We played, and fought every day till I had to go sot [set] the table. I was so small I had to get in a chair to get the dishes out of the safe. I had to pull a long fly brush over the table while the white fo'ks et.

Master lived there in Jefferson, but had a farm 'bout four miles from town. He had a overseer that rode a horse over the farm. I'se seed him buckle the Niggers cross a log and whip them. Master Bill run a big livery stable there in Jefferson. When he went to the farm he allus [always] took his boy with him. We would be out in the barn playing and Master would call from the house, "Come on, Jimmie, we is going to the farm." Jimmie allus wanted me to go too. He say to me, "Come on, little Nigger, lets ride round the farm." I say to him, "I ain't no Nigger." He say to me, "Yes you is, my Pa paid $200.00 for you. He bought you for to play with me." . . .

I was in Jefferson during the War, and seed the Yankees soldiers all dressed in blue when they come to run the town at the close of the War. The Federates brought soldiers there on boats twice. I think 'fore war ceased. We could hear the fighting and cannons shooting during the War, but I didn't know where they was.

I 'members Master telling me I was free, but I stayed on with him till I was most grown. I worked round town for a while, then married Dave Black. We moved to a farm in Cass County. I raised six chil'ren. My ole man got so trifling and mean that I quit him and worked for myself. After I quit my man I come to Texarkana. I allus could earn my own living till 'about a year ago I lost my seeing and Albert Ragland took me in his home for old fo'ks. They gives me a $10.00 per month pension now.

From The American Slave: A Composite Autobiography, vol. 2, Texas Narratives, Part I, *George Rawick (ed.), Greenwood Press, 1979.*

Chapter 32
A MAN WITH A CONSCIENCE

On the back of the monument at Sam Houston's grave are these words:

Soldier under Jackson; Boy Hero of Horseshoe Bend; Congressman from Tennessee; Governor of Tennessee; Chief of the Cherokees; Commander-in-Chief of the Texas Army; Hero of San Jacinto; Twice President of the Texas Republic; United States Senator; Governor of Texas.

On the front of the statue appear these words:

The world will take care of Houston's fame.

—Andrew Jackson

As both a U.S. senator and governor of the new state of Texas, Sam was fiercely opposed to the Southern secessionist movement. He was deposed from the governorship for refusing to take the oath of allegiance to the Confederacy. Jeff Hamilton, a former slave and personal valet to Sam Houston, gives us his first-person account of those difficult days.

President Lincoln is said to have offered Sam Houston the use of federal troops to keep him in the governor's office and Texas in the Union (Martin Johnson Heade, *Sam Houston*, oil, 1847, Archives and Information Services Division, Texas State Library, Austin).

At last, the day came upon which Mr. Lincoln was elected our president.

For some months I had noticed that my master [Sam Houston] was aging fast. At times he would walk with a crutch, and used his cane all the time now. But his eyes were clear, and his mind as keen and sharp as ever. He was almost sixty-eight early in 1860. His old wounds, which I had dressed hundreds of times, were paining him more than usual, especially during the cold, damp winter months. . . .

It was on January 28 that the State Convention of Secession met at Austin, in the capitol building. They drew up an ordinance of secession without wasting any time, and set February 1 as the date for the delegates to vote on it. Just before twelve o'clock noon that day, the Convention decided to ask the General [Houston] to appear before it. They knew that nearly every one of the delegates was for secession and that the General couldn't change a single vote at that late date. But they wanted to show him a courtesy on account of his long fight for Texas independence and annexation and all he had done for the State.

A committee of six members was appointed to ask my master to appear before them. . . .

The General accepted the invitation, and I hurried to bring him his coat and hat, also giving him his comb and brush to tidy up his hair. But he did not wear his hat. I followed my master and the committee up the stairs, but they hurried into the House of Representatives, and someone slammed the door in my face. But I had made up my mind nothing would keep me from the room. I ran up the stairway that opened into the balcony, and managed to get in without anyone seeing me. I crawled behind one of the posts where I could see and hear everything but where I could not be seen from the floor of the house. . . .

The General was given the seat of honor beside Judge Oran M. Roberts . . . who was then chief justice of the supreme court.

My master rose to speak. You could have heard a pin drop. I can remember only a few of the things he said, but I best remember how he said them and how he acted. He began by saying:

"All of you know that I am opposed to secession, and all of you know my convictions on the subject. I have taken an oath to support the Constitution of the United States and its flag and the Constitution of Texas and its flag. I almost died fighting for that flag, and I almost died fighting for the Texas flag. I have served Texas under both of those flags for a long time. Gentlemen, you cannot forget those two flags—you cannot withdraw from the Union.

"The country is just now in a state of prosperity. To secede from the Union and set up another government would cause war. I advise you to remain in the Union. For, if you go to war with the United States, you will never conquer her, as she has the money and the men. If she does not whip you by guns, powder, and steel, she will starve you to death. Now, if you go to war, it will take the flower of the country—the young men. I know what war is. I have been in it often and do not want any more of it. War is no plaything and this war will be a bloody war. There will be thousands and thousands who march away from our homes never to come back. There will be numberless mothers and children made widows and orphans. I advise you to settle this matter peaceably. Where there is union there is strength, and if you break the Union you will wreck the whole fabric of the Constitution. No, I will never agree to sign Texas away as a seceding state."

At this point in his speech, my master's voice choked with emotion, and tears—the biggest tears I ever saw in my life—rolled down his cheeks.

"I will show you the wounds I received in fighting for Texas and the Union you would destroy," added my master. And then my master placed his hand on his right thigh, bared his right arm, and pointed down to his ankle, and said:

"A barbed Indian arrow struck that thigh. I will take that wound to my grave. It has never healed. This arm and shoulder were shattered by Indian rifle balls. My ankle was broken to pieces at San Jacinto," he concluded and limped to his seat.

There was a deep silence, when Colonel Rogers rose and asked the General:

"Well, Sam, do you believe that your wife and daughters ought to scrub their clothes at a wash-tub and cook meals in pots over a hot fire? Before I would suffer my wife and daughter to cook and scrub, I'll wade in blood up to my neck!"

My master answered that washing and scrubbing were honorable and that no white woman had ever died from honorable work.

Then, Mr. Montgomery got up and raised a secession flag over the General's head, and asked him if he would rather give up the governor's office or join the secession plan.

My master answered:

"The reason I wanted to be governor of this state was to help it on its feet, and now everybody seems to be getting along nicely. I am not particular about the office. I have a home and livestock and can live without the office. . . . No, I will never give up the Constitution or the Union."

The convention then voted to adopt the Ordinance of Secession, which carried by a vote of 174 to 7 votes. The ordinance was then submitted to a vote of the people . . . and the vote was 46,129 for secession to 14,697 against secession. March 5 was the day fixed for Texas to join the Confederate nation, and March 16 the time for state officials to take the oath of office.

On the latter date, the secretary of the convention began to call the roll of state officials, so that each one of them might take the oath of allegiance. . . . The first name called was that of "Sam Houston." The General had stayed away on purpose, and after his name was called several times, his office was declared vacant, and Mr. Edward Clark, the lieutenant governor, was sworn in as governor. . . . My master had ended his long public career. . . .

Having given up the office of governor of Texas rather than to take an oath against his conscience, the General got ready to leave Austin. Within a few days, Uncle Joshua started several wagons ahead, loaded with household goods, including barrels of glassware and ornaments, and several boxes of books and papers which the General always carried with him from place to place.

Then, Tom Blue drove the great yellow coach and its four horses up to the entrance of the governor's mansion. Soon, it was on its way with Mrs. Houston, the children and the colored maids. The rest of the Negroes followed in a wagon. . . .

I waited with the top buggy for the General, who was seeing some friends in the business part of town before leaving. When he came, we found a large amount of papers and other things which had been overlooked, and crammed them in the buggy and headed east.

Nobody will ever know how bad I felt about my master losing his office as governor. I felt that all of us were disgraced by the way the secessionists had practically thrown him out of the capitol. . . .

I felt like the end of the world had come, but my spirits began to revive when I saw the grand way my master was hiding the grief I knew he must be suffering every time he thought about his own Texas leaving the Union and his fear that the Union would be wrecked. I was old enough now to have a pretty good idea of what was causing the war which everybody knew would start any time. I could also have some idea of the terrible suffering that would come with it.

From My Master: The Inside Story of Sam Houston and His Times by His Former Slave, Jeff Hamilton, Lenoir Hunt, State House Press, 1992. Reprinted courtesy of State House Press.

References

The chapter listing in parentheses following the source information refers to the chapter in which the source material was used.

MANUSCRIPTS

Bailey, James B. Biographical File. Archives, Center for American History, University of Texas, Austin. (Chapter 23)

Crockett, David. Papers. The Alamo, San Antonio. (Chapter 5)

Dresel, Julius. Notebook, San Antonio Public Library, San Antonio. (Chapter 24)

Herff, Charles Adelbert. Papers. Archives, Center for American History, University of Texas, Austin. (Chapter 30)

Hornsby, Reuben. Papers. Archives Division, Texas State Library, Austin. (Chapter 8)

Sinks, Julia Lee. Papers. Archives, Center for American History, University of Texas, Austin. (Chapter 15)

Wallace, William Alexander Anderson. Papers. Archives, Center for American History, University of Texas, Austin. (Chapter 12)

BOOKS AND PAMPHLETS

Baker, D. W. C. A Texas Scrap-book: Made up of the History, Biography, and Miscellany of Texas and Its People. Austin: Texas State Historical Association, 1991. (Chapter 9)

Bandelier, Fanny (trans.). The Journey of Alvar Núñez Cabeza de Vaca. New York: A. S. Barnes, 1905. Reprinted by the Rio Grande Press. (Chapter 1)

Cade, Winifred. Think Back: Being the Memoirs of Grandma Gruen. San Antonio: Privately printed, 1937. (Reprinted in Crystal Ragsdale, The Golden Free Land. Austin: Landmark Press, 1976; and Jo Ella Powell Exley, Texas Tears and Texas Sunshine: Voices of Frontier Women. College Station: Texas A & M University Press, 1985). (Chapter 18)

Dobie, J. Frank (ed.). Legends of Texas. Vol. 2, Pirate's Gold and Other Tales. Gretna: Pelican Publishing, 1924. (Chapter 3)

Duval, John C. *The Adventures of Big Foot Wallace.* Macon, Georgia: J. W. Burke & Co., 1970. (Chapter 12)

Eisen, Jonathan, and Harold Straughn (eds.). *Unknown Texas.* New York: Macmillan, 1988. (Chapter 1)

Exley, Jo Ella Powell (ed.). *Texas Tears and Texas Sunshine: Voices of Frontier Women.* College Station: Texas A & M University Press, 1985. (Chapters 4, 10, 18)

Green, Rena Maverick. *Memoirs of Mary Maverick.* Lincoln: University of Nebraska Press, 1989. (Chapter 6)

Helm, Mary Sherwood. *Scraps of Early Texas History.* Austin: Privately printed, 1884. (Reprinted in Jo Ella Powell Exley, *Texas Tears and Texas Sunshine: Voices of Frontier Women.* College Station: Texas A & M University Press, 1985). (Chapter 4)

Hodge, Frederick W. (ed.). *Spanish Explorers in the Southern United States, 1528–1543.* Austin: Texas State Historical Association, 1990. (Chapter 1)

Hogan, William Ransom. *The Texas Republic: A Social and Economic History.* Norman: University of Oklahoma Press, 1946. (Chapters 19, 21)

Hunt, Lenoir. *My Master: The Inside Story of Sam Houston and His Times by His Former Slave, Jeff Hamilton.* Austin: State House Press, 1992. (Chapter 32)

Jackson, Grace. *Cynthia Ann Parker.* San Antonio: Naylor, 1959. (Chapter 29)

Jenkins, John Holmes III (ed.). *Recollections of Early Texas: The Memoirs of John Holland Jenkins.* Austin: University of Texas Press, 1958. (Chapter 11)

Laffite, Jean. *The Journal of Jean Laffite: The Privateer-Patriot's Own Story.* New York: Vantage Press, 1958. (Chapter 3)

Nathan, Paul D. (trans.), and Lesley Byrd Simpson (ed.). *The San Saba Papers (A Documentary Account of the Founding and Destruction of San Saba Mission).* San Francisco: John Howell Books, 1959. (Chapter 2)

Olmsted, Frederick Law. *A Journey Through Texas. Or, A Saddle-Trip on the Southwestern Frontier.* Austin: University of Texas Press, 1989. (Chapters 16, 17, 27)

Pratt, Willis W. (ed.). *Galveston Island. Or, A Few Months Off the Coast of Texas: The Journal of Francis C. Sheridan, 1839–1840.* Austin: University of Texas Press, 1954. (Chapter 25)

Rawick, George (ed.). *The American Slave: A Composite Autobiography.* Vol. 2, *Texas Narratives,* Part 1. Connecticut: Greenwood Press, 1979. (Chapter 31)

Smithwick, Noah. *Evolution of a State.* Austin: University of Texas Press, 1983. (Chapters 7, 10, 13, 14)

Waugh, Julia Nott. *Castro-Ville and Henry Castro, Empresario.* San Antonio: Standard Printing, 1934. (Chapter 22)

PERIODICALS

Cates, T. J. "Cynthia Ann Parker," *Edgewood Journal,* June, 1918. (Reprinted in Grace Jackson, *Cynthia Ann Parker.* San Antonio: Naylor, 1959. (Chapter 29)

"Crockett Had Great Faith in Texas," *Fort Worth Press,* 7 March, 1936. (Chapter 5)

"Life in Eastern Texas—Dancing to a Strange Tune," New Orleans *Daily Picayune* 11 March 1843. (Chapter 21)

Patten, Roderick, "Miranda's Inspection of Los Almagres: His Journal, Report, and Petition," *Southwestern Historical Quarterly,* Vol. 74 (1970–1971): 223–254. (Chapter 2)

"Pioneer Tells Graphic Story of Wild Horse Catching Fifty Years Ago in Texas," *Fort Worth Star-Telegram,* 27 February 1941, evening edition. (Chapter 28)

"The Reminiscences of Mrs. Dilue Rose Harris," *Quarterly of the Texas State Historical Association,* Vols. 4 (1900): 85–127, 155–189; 7 (1904): 214–222. (Reprinted in Jo Ella Powell Exley, *Texas Tears and Texas Sunshine: Voices of Frontier Women.* College Station: Texas A & M University Press, 1985). (Chapter 10)

Wade, Amzina, "Recollections of a Child's Life on a Pioneer Plantation," *Chronicles of Smith County, Texas,* Vol. 19, No. 2 (winter 1980): 45–54. (Chapter 26)

Walsh, Captain W. C., "Austin in the Making," *The Austin Statesman,* 3 February 1924. (Chapter 20)

Index

E

Eagle Pass (Tex), 75
Eagleville Colony, 16-17
English immigrants, 109-110

F

fandango, Mexican, 97-99
Flacco, Chief, 69
food: Carancahua, 4, 5;
    Comanche, 62, 125; French,
    81; (for) hogs, 111, (for)
    horny toads, 110; on ship,
    17-19; wild game, 115-116;
    Lipan Apache, 70; Mexican,
    76, 97, 99; pioneer, 41, 77,
    79, 80, 84, 91; plantation
    sausage-making, 111-113;
    ring-tailed roarers, 101;
    slaves, 137; Tonkawas, 26,
    65, 67
French immigrants, 16-17, 68,
    78, 81, 97
Fox, William, 92
Fredericksburg (Tex), 83-84,
    114-117
freebooters, 30
Frételèire, Auguste, 97

G

Galveston Bay, 11
Galveston Island, 3-5, 10
Galveston (Tex), 109-110
Gentilz, Théodore, 68, 97-98
German immigrants, 80-81,
    83-84, 104-106, 113-117
ghosts, 11-14
gold, 3, 8, 11, 106
Gold Rush, California, 106
Goliad (Tex), 26, 55
government, 22, 55-56, 139-144
"G.T.T.", 63
Guadalupe River, 105
Gulf Coast, 49
Gulf of Mexico, 3,10, 11, 17-19,
    21

H

Haggett, Mr., 31-35
Hamilton, Jeff, 139
hangings, 128-134
Harris, Dilue Rose, 43
Hays, John Coffee (Jack), 83
Helm, Mary Wightman, 17
Henry, O., 48

wagons, 17, 24-27, 75, 85, 90, 135, 143-144. *See also* animals: horses; animals: mules; art in chapter openers.

Travis, William Barrett, 39-40, 83

Trinity River, 16-17, 44-47

V

vigilantes, 49-52, 128-134

W

Walcart, Major, 11

Wallace, William Alexander Anderson (Big Foot), 53-54

Watts, Mrs., 50, 52

whooping cough, 44

Williams, Mr., 31-35

work: Carancahuas, 4-5; Comanche women, 125-126; farm, 105; pioneer men, 85-86, 91, 115-117, 118-122; pioneer women, 82-84, 85, 91; plantation, 111-113; ranching, 114; slave, 135-138, 139, 141, 143-144

women: Carancahua, 4-5; Comanche, 62,125; Mexican, 99; pioneer, 82-84, 85-87, 91-92, 117

Y

yellow fever (yellow jack), 25, 83